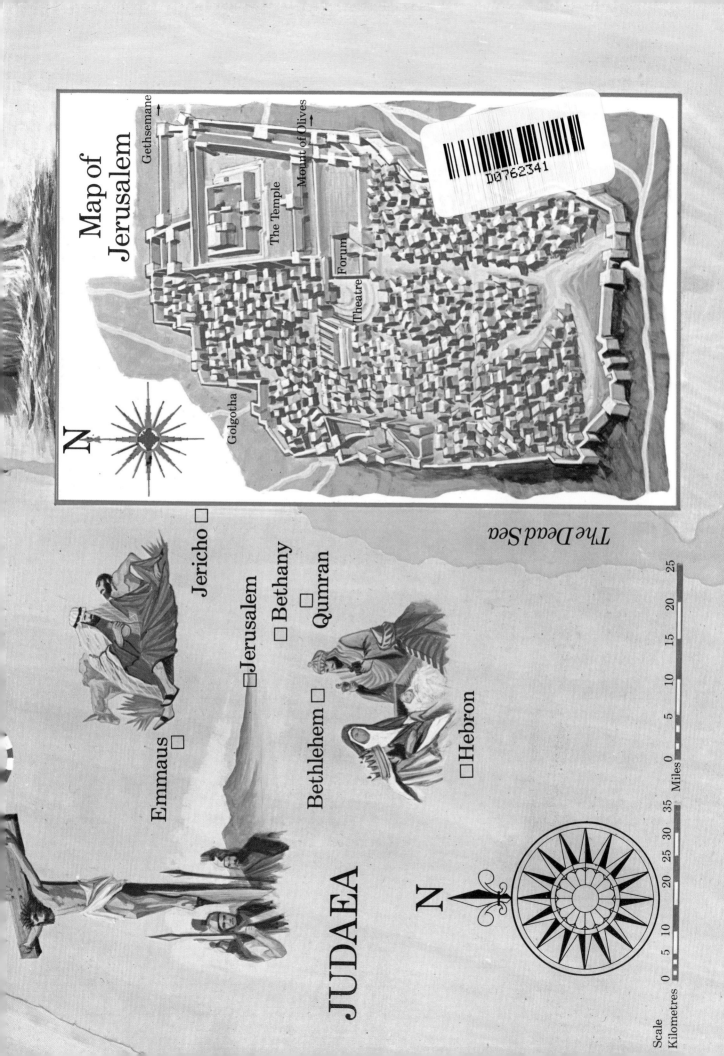

Map of Jerusalem

Gethsemane

Mount of Olives

The Temple

Forum

Theatre

Golgotha

N

The Dead Sea

Jericho

Emmaus

Jerusalem

Bethany

Qumran

Bethlehem

Hebron

JUDAEA

N

Scale

Kilometres   0   5   10   20   25   30   35   Miles

0   5   10   15   20   25

To: Garth Buhr

Participation in the
"Island In The Son" 1990

Camp Director
Yvone Jones

The Story of Jesus

Norman J. Bull

illustrated by Mike Codd

Life in the Time of Jesus
illustrated by Gerald Witcomb
Peter Dennis and Roger Hall

Abingdon
Nashville

The Story of Jesus

*The story of Jesus is told in the four Gospels of the New
Testament. The drama of his life and the parables by which he
taught are told in simple and beautiful and moving language.
But life in the time of Jesus was very different from life in our
twentieth century. Jesus spoke to his people of everyday things
in the world they knew — not of everyday things in the world we
know. Jesus spoke in familiar everyday terms — not in our
language and thought-forms. Nor were the parables of Jesus
just simple stories that could be easily understood. People had
to search in them for the 'heavenly meaning' that would
challenge their minds and stir their hearts.*

*In this book we want to bring to life the world of Jesus and his
teaching. Thus it tells of the contemporary ways and customs
which lie behind the Gospel Story. It gives contemporary names
to help bring alive such characters in that story as 'a certain
man', 'my little daughter', 'the younger son' and 'the elder son'.
In such ways this book seeks to fill in the background of the life
and teaching of Jesus.*

*The aim of this book is therefore that the reader may turn to the
Gospels themselves and find a deeper understanding of their
story of Jesus.*

Published 1980 by
The Hamlyn Publishing Group Limited
London · New York · Sydney · Toronto
Astronaut House, Feltham, Middlesex, England
© Copyright The Hamlyn Publishing Group Limited 1980

U.S. edition 1982 by Abingdon
Second impression 1984

ISBN 0-687-39659 X

Printed in Spain by Graficromo, S.A., Córdoba

Contents

The birth of Jesus

TWO THOUSAND YEARS AGO, in the land of Israel, there lived a man named Joseph, and a woman named Mary. They dwelt in the little town of Nazareth, cradled in the hills of Galilee. Israel had been the homeland of the Jews from ancient times. Now it had been conquered by the Romans, and it was part of the mighty Roman empire. Jews hated their conquerors, and they longed to be free. Some plotted against the Romans, and raised revolts against them. Devout Jews, like Joseph and Mary, put their trust in God. He would send a Savior to his chosen people. The Savior would set up God's kingdom among them, and reign over them in peace and righteousness.

Joseph was a carpenter of Nazareth. In his workshop he made chests and furniture for people's homes, and yokes and ploughs for their farms. He helped to build houses, too. Everyone knew Joseph as a good man, whose work was always well done.

Joseph was engaged to marry a devout girl named Mary. Their engagement would last for a whole year, and then would come the joyful week of wedding festivities. Now the bride would go to her husband's house, and they would make their home together. But, long before the wedding time, Mary had a vision: she

8

had been chosen by God to be the mother of the promised Savior. And Mary rejoiced that God had blessed her, above all other women, to serve him in this wonderful way.

Joseph was troubled when he found that his future wife was with child. But he, too, was told in a dream that God had chosen Mary, and blessed her. Her child would be a son—the Savior sent by God to his people. Then Joseph took Mary into his home straightaway, as his wife. And they lived together in great happiness, waiting for the coming of her child.

Bethlehem

It was nearly time for Mary's baby to be born when Joseph had to make a journey. Caesar Augustus, the great emperor of Rome, had ordered a census to be made of all the people in this part of his empire. This counting of the people was made by the Romans every 14 years, so that they could tax the people they ruled. Everyone knew this, and hated it. But even worse was the rule that everyone had to go back to the place he came from, to be enrolled by the Romans.

Joseph came from the tribe of the great King David, which had lived far away in the south. So he had to travel to Bethlehem, the ancient home of King David, 84 miles away from his home at Nazareth.

The name Bethlehem means 'House of Bread', for the land around it grew good corn for making bread. The little town lay in the hills, over 4 miles south of Jerusalem. Inside its ancient wall there were narrow, jumbled streets, and white-washed houses with flat roofs, packed tight together. The town was more crowded than ever with people who had come back for the counting. One ordinary house had been turned into an inn. It was soon packed out with visitors who spread their mattresses all over the floor.

Joseph was troubled as he led his donkey into Bethlehem, with Mary on its back. For her time was near, and he was anxious to find her a resting-place. The innkeeper was a gruff man, but he had a kindly heart.

'No room at the inn!' he said roughly. Then he looked at Mary. 'Make a bed in the stable, if you like. Plenty of clean straw there.'

So Joseph found shelter for Mary in the cave under the inn, used as a stable. And there she brought forth her firstborn son. His name had been decided long before, when she had her vision. It was to be JESUS, which means GOD SAVES.

Shepherds

Baby Jesus was washed, and rubbed with salt to harden the skin, as the custom was. Then he was folded in a

9

square cloth, and swaddled with strips of linen, wrapped around him like bandages. They would help his limbs to grow straight. They fastened his hands to his sides, so that he could not move. Now he could be laid in one of the stone mangers, safe and cosy and warm in the clean straw. Only the oxen and asses, tied to their mangers, were there to greet the newborn Savior. But soon there were others.

Out on the lonely hills around Bethlehem there were shepherds, guarding their precious sheep from crafty jackals and cunning foxes. Their flocks were safe for the night inside the stone walls of the fold. The shepherds lay across the opening, so that no wild beast could enter. Above them the clear blue sky sparkled with twinkling stars.

Then, suddenly, came dazzling light. It filled the sky, as with the glory of God. And a voice came to the terrified shepherds: 'Fear not! I bring tidings of great joy! This day, in the city of David, the Savior is born! You will find him in Bethlehem, lying in a manger!'

Then as the voice ceased there came the swelling sound of heavenly music, as if the dazzling light was a great choir of angels singing the praises of God.

The music died away, the vision of light faded, and the shepherds were alone. They turned to each other in astonishment.

'What does it mean?' asked one.

'Let's go to Bethlehem and see,' said another.

'Yes!' they all agreed. 'Let's go to Bethlehem!'

Quickly they filled the entrance to the fold with a hedge of sturdy branches, thickened with sharp-thorned brushwood, and hurried down the hillside to Bethlehem. They came to the inn, and saw the glimmer of light from the stable. Quietly they tiptoed inside. There they saw Joseph, and Mary, and the babe in swaddling clothes lying in the manger—just as the voice had said. And they sank to their knees in wonder at all that had come to pass.

Wise men

The Jews were not the only people looking for the coming of a Savior. In faraway Persia there were priests of the stars, called Magi. These wise men studied the heavenly bodies which, they believed, ruled over the earth and ordered the lives of men. From the stars they foretold the future. The stars would tell them when the heavenly King came to earth.

One night they saw a brilliant new star in the sky. The time had come—the star would guide them to the newborn King. Three of the Magi left everything to follow it. They took with them the most precious gifts of all. Mile after mile their camel train plodded through the sandy deserts of Arabia, following the famous Incense Road of the merchants. The star led them to Jerusalem, and there they asked where the new King had been born.

Old King Herod grew mad with suspicion when he heard of the travellers from afar, and their search for a new King. He sent for the Chief Priests of the Jews.

'Where is your promised Savior supposed to be born?' he asked.

11

'In Bethlehem, the city of David,' they said. 'That is what our prophets foretell, in the holy writings.'

Then Herod sent for the wise men secretly.

'Go and search in Bethlehem for your newborn King,' he said. 'When you find him come and tell me. Then I can go and worship him too.'

The wise men followed the star till it stood still over the town of Bethlehem. There they sought eagerly, and came at last to the goal of their long journey. They knelt down and worshipped Jesus, and offered their precious gifts. The first offered gold, the symbol of a king. The second offered incense, the costly gum, white and scented, used to make holy oil. It was a symbol of worship and of holiness. The third offered myrrh, the yellow, scented gum used for anointing the dead. It was a symbol of suffering and of death.

The travellers set off on their long journey home. But they went by another road, for they had been warned in a dream not to return to the treacherous Herod.

Mary and Joseph, too, began their journey back to Nazareth. They had to pass through Jerusalem, the holy city of the Jews, on their way. There, in the sacred Temple, baby Jesus was offered to God in the ceremony of dedication. For the firstborn of every living creature belonged to God—especially a firstborn son, the greatest joy of all to a Jewish family. But the old priest, Simeon, taking Jesus in his arms, knew that this was no ordinary child. He praised God that he had lived long enough to behold the promised Savior.

Then Joseph took Mary and her child back to their home at Nazareth. And there Jesus grew up.

Christmas

For two thousand years the followers of Jesus have kept a happy festival to remember the birth of Jesus. They are called Christians, for they believe that Jesus is the CHRIST—the Savior sent by God to mankind. And Christmas is the birthday of Jesus.

In lands of the West, Christians keep his birthday on 25 December. In lands of the East Christmas is kept by some Christians on 9 January and by others on 19 January. These differences do not matter. What matters to all Christians is to have one special day in the year to thank God for the birth of the Savior.

Mary, too, has always been honored as the mother of Jesus. Her Jewish name, *Myriam,* means *Beloved of God.* In Greek and Latin it became *Maria* which means *The Lady.* That is why some Christians call her *Our Lady*—which in French is *Notre Dame,* and in Italian is *Madonna.* For they honor Mary as the mother of their Savior.

12

The boy Jesus

ARLY ONE BRIGHT SPRING MORNING Jesus stood on the hilltop near his home. It was like standing on top of the world. Far below, in the cradle of the hills, was the little town of Nazareth where he lived. Away to the north he could see snow-capped Mount Hermon, its white peak glistening in the sun. On the east the river Jordan twisted like a snake through its valley, and the Sea of Galilee gleamed like a huge mirror. To the west he could see as far as Mount Carmel which reared up out of the Great Sea.

Best of all was the view to the south, where he looked down on the fine Roman road which ran right through the land of Israel. Many a day he stood here and watched travellers passing by: merchants, with their caravan of camels swaying under heavy burdens; Roman soldiers marching past, with tramping feet and clinking armour; rulers and princes, guarded by horsemen trotting beside their chariots; and sometimes just a lonely traveller, staff in hand, walking beside his loaded donkey.

But today was a special day, the greatest day Jesus had ever known. For now he was 12 years old, and he himself was to be a traveller. He was leaving home for the very first time. He was going to the most important city in the whole world – Jerusalem, the city of God.

Pilgrims from Nazareth

Soon Jesus was hurrying down the hill, running through the street, dashing into his house. Eagerly he washed and dressed, taking from the family chest the fine new tunic and girdle which his mother Mary had made specially for this day. Mary and Joseph too were in their best clothes for the pilgrimage to Jerusalem.

They had a quick breakfast together – home-made bread, figs and olives, and goat's milk to drink. Then they loaded the family donkey with all the things needed for their journey – tent, mattresses, cooking-pots, water-bottles, and plenty of food. For the journey of 78 miles would take them three days, with all the fun of camping by the road when night came swiftly on.

Patient donkeys waited outside other houses too. For many families were going as pilgrims to Jerusalem at this time. It was the greatest time of the whole year – the festival of Passover. Jews came from all over the world to keep the Passover at the Temple of Jerusalem. They came to thank God for saving their people from slavery in Egypt, long ago; for bringing them into the land which he had promised them; and for making them his chosen people.

There were friends of Jesus among the pilgrims from Nazareth. They were the boys who had been with him at school. Girls were taught by their mothers at home. Boys went to school at the synagogue when they were six years old. At school Jesus and his friends had learned to read the Bible of their people — the sacred writings which told the whole story of God and his people. Now they were 12 years old, and schooldays were over. Now they were ready to take their place among the people of God. Now they were old enough to take part in his worship, to keep his sacred laws, and to live by his commandments.

Camping at night

At last everyone was ready. The happy pilgrims set off with their long caravan of donkeys quite hidden under their heavy loads. They kept close together, for bands of robbers lurked in the rocky hills, on the look-out for lonely and defenseless travellers.

When the sun rose high the pilgrims stopped for food and drink, and rested during the heat of the day. Then on again, till the sun began to sink behind the hills, and a place must be found for their night camp. Donkeys were unloaded, fed and watered; tents were set up; camp fires were lit; and soon the delicious smell of cooking brought families together for supper. It was the best meal of the day, and Mary had made a delicious stew with onions and beans and lentils.

After supper and prayers Jesus snuggled down on his mattress. But he was too excited to sleep much that night.

The road to Jerusalem

The pilgrims were up at dawn, hurrying over breakfast so as to be on the road before the sun grew hot.

By now families were mixing together, especially the children. Jesus was with his friends most of the day. Mary was not at all worried, for all the families were relatives or friends from Nazareth, and Jesus would be quite safe.

The road they were taking ran southwards, along the

valley of the river Jordan, twisting and turning with the snaking river. They passed by small villages and tiny hamlets on their journey, with more and more pilgrims joining them on the road to Jerusalem.

By nightfall they reached the ancient town of Jericho. It was a well-watered city, just like an oasis in the desert with its leafy trees of palms and dates and bananas. There they camped for the night, knowing that the new day would bring them to their goal, the holy city of Jerusalem.

The holy city

Soon after dawn they were on their way, climbing the rocky, sun-scorched road that led to the village of Bethany, outside Jerusalem. After Bethany came the most exciting part of their journey. The road went downhill, twisting and turning, and parents had told their children that at one of its bends they would see Jerusalem. The boys raced ahead, each hoping to be the first to see it.

Then at last – there it was! Facing them, high on its hill, was the holy city, surrounded by mighty walls, its white-washed houses shimmering in the sunlight. Above them all towered the beautiful Temple, its white marble, inlaid with gold, glistening as if with the glory of God. Jesus and his friends stood silent, open-mouthed with wonder at such a vision of beauty.

The Father's house

Now the donkeys clip-clopped down the hill, over the brook, and up the steep slope to the city walls. But the sound of their hooves was drowned by the joyful songs of praise that rose up from the happy pilgrims. The boys had learned these psalms at school, of course, and they joined in with all their hearts. Soon they were moving through the crowded streets, till the Temple stood before them in all its glory.

They passed in silent wonder through the courts of the great Temple. The Temple itself rang with the stirring sound of trumpets, the music of harps and drums and clashing cymbals, the singing of choirs, the chanting of priests, the hallelujahs of the people.

It seemed so natural to Jesus to be there. This was his Father's house. Now he was at home.

Jerusalem was packed with pilgrims from all over the world, during the week of the Passover festival. The pilgrims from Nazareth camped on the hill outside the city each night. Every morning Jesus and his friends went into the Temple courtyard to meet the great Rabbis, teachers of the law of God. They questioned the boys on what they had learned at school, and discussed with them the holy writings and their teaching.

Mary and Joseph did not see much of Jesus during the daytime. They took it for granted that Jesus was with his friends. But often Jesus stayed with the Rabbis, long after the others had gone, eagerly asking questions and listening to their wise sayings.

Jesus is lost

All too soon came the end of the festival. Now it was time for the journey back home. The pilgrims from Nazareth loaded up their donkeys, and soon their long caravan was on the road back to Jericho. The children had lots of exciting things to talk about, so Mary was not worried about Jesus not being with her and Joseph. She was sure he would be safe with friends.

But it was different when they made camp for the night, near Jericho, and Mary began to look for Jesus. 'No, he's not with us,' said one family after another. Mary grew more and more troubled. Jesus was nowhere to be found. They must go back and search for him.

At sunrise Mary and Joseph hurried back to Jerusalem. They asked everyone they knew in the city. For three days they searched high and low, frantic with worry. There was no trace of Jesus. Then in despair Mary went back to the Temple courtyard – perhaps the Rabbis might know something that could help them.

There were the Rabbis – and there was Jesus, sitting calmly before them.

Something in Mary snapped. All her fear and worry burst into a flame of anger.

'Jesus!' she cried, as she hurried to him. 'How could you treat us like this! Joseph and I have been searching everywhere for you! Didn't you realize that we'd be worried to death about you?'

Jesus was astonished.

'But why did you go round looking for me, Mother? Didn't you realize that I would be in my Father's house?' he said calmly.

Mary bit her lip, keeping back angry words welling up inside her. Sometimes it was so hard to understand Jesus. He was a strange boy. One of the first words that she had taught him was the child's name for God – Abba, that is, Daddy. And often Jesus seemed so close to his heavenly Father – and so far from his parents.

But Jesus was a real boy, and he grew into a fine young man. He went back to Nazareth with Mary and Joseph, and he was always kind and dutiful to them. From Joseph he learned the craft of a carpenter, and toiled with him in the workshop.

But Mary never forgot. And she knew in her heart that Jesus had much greater work to do, when his time came.

Jesus is tempted

ESUS WAS ABOUT 30 YEARS OLD when the time came. Since he was a boy he had lived at Nazareth, and worked as a carpenter. His time had been spent in making yokes and ploughs for the farm, chests and stools and cradles for the home, and doors and roof-beams and window-frames for houses. Now the time had come to leave his home and his work at Nazareth, and to begin his work for God. Why had it come now?

Jesus had a cousin named John, the son of an old priest. John's parents had dedicated him to the service of God. When John grew up he knew that he had a special work to do. He cared nothing for food, or clothes, or comfort. He went out to live a hard life in the cruel wilderness. His only food was wild honey, and the grasshoppers called locusts. His only dress was a rough cloak, made from the skin of a camel, to protect him from the burning heat of day and the bitter cold of night. His only companions were lizards and scorpions, the birds of prey called vultures, and the poisonous snakes called vipers.

Each day John went to a place where travellers had to wade across the river Jordan. This ford was on the main road from north to south. So it was a fine place to meet the people, and to speak to them for God. The news spread like wildfire – a new prophet had arisen in Israel! For 400 years there had been no prophet to proclaim the message of God to his people. No wonder that people flocked out from towns and villages to hear him.

Who could he be? That was the question everyone was asking. Could John be the Savior, promised by God through the prophets of old?

The baptism of Jesus

John was a wild man, with his rough dress, his mane of fiery hair, his flashing eyes, his thundering voice. His words were fierce and frightening. He told the people of God's anger with them, not of God's love for them. Their only hope was to be sorry for their evil ways, to come down into the water and be washed of their sins against God.

Some people laughed and sneered at John. 'He's just a madman,' they said. 'He's got a devil inside him.' But others believed that his message was from God. They came humbly to the water to be baptized by John, to have their evil washed away, and to begin a new life with God.

There was something new in John's words. People kept asking, 'Who are you?'

John said, 'I am a herald. You know how a slave runs before a royal procession shouting, "Clear the road! Make way for the King!" That is what I am. I am preparing the way for one who comes after me. He is far, far greater than I. I am not worthy even to kneel down and untie his sandals.'

Then some people remembered the ancient belief that the great prophet Elijah would come back to earth. He would be the herald of the Savior. Didn't John look like Elijah, live like him, and speak like him?

One day, when John had finished speaking, he went down to the water to baptize those who came to him. There, before him, stood his cousin Jesus.

John was amazed. 'Why do you come to me?' he asked humbly. 'I am the one who needs to be washed, not you. You should baptize me.'

'It is the will of God,' said Jesus.

So Jesus was baptized by John in the river Jordan. And Jesus felt the Spirit of God upon him, like a dove settling gently on his shoulder. And he heard within him the voice of his Father – 'You are my only Son.'

John was glad that Jesus had come to him. It meant that his work had not been in vain. Jesus had shown that John was indeed his herald.

Later on there came the time when John was cruelly put to death by the evil son of King Herod. When Jesus heard the terrible news he spoke about John.

'There never lived a greater man than John,' he said. 'For he was the herald, preparing the way – the Elijah who was to come.'

Turn stones to bread!

After the wonderful experience at his baptism Jesus went out into the wilderness. He had to be alone. He had always known that God was within him – that he was the Savior promised to his people. Now his time had come. He had to decide once and for all. What kind of Savior would he be?

It was a hard struggle. The Spirit of God was with him. But there was a spirit of evil, too, whom Jews called Satan, which means Enemy. And out in the lonely wilderness Jesus was tempted by Satan. This was how Jesus described it later to his friends.

Jesus sat alone in the wilderness, a bleak desert of rocks and stones. Satan came to him and said, 'If you really are the Son of God, you must have the power of God within you. You must be able to do anything.

20

All right — prove it! Command these stones to turn into loaves of bread!'

Now Jesus was fasting, going without food and drink, in the barren wilderness. How tempting the thought of food was, in his hunger!

But this temptation was not just about his own hunger. Jesus had grown up in a poor, peasant home. He knew how hard it was for poor people to feed and clothe their children, and to provide a home for them. That was not all. They had to pay taxes twice over – their own Jewish taxes, and the taxes demanded by the Romans. **How they would welcome a Savior who would save** them from grinding poverty, and give them plenty. Jesus answered Satan with words from the holy writings:

'Men do not live by bread alone. They need food for their souls, as well as food for their bodies.'

Jesus would not win men by bringing them food and plenty. That was not the way to win their hearts. That was not God's way.

21

Throw yourself down!

Again Satan tempted Jesus. His mind floated away, and
he saw himself at the Temple of Jerusalem, with Satan
by his side. They were on the highest turret, right at the
top of the great building. It jutted out almost 100 feet
above the valley far, far below. And there Satan
tempted him:

'Throw yourself down, if you really are the Son of
God! That would prove it to everyone! The angels of God
will bear you up, as your Bible promises. What a miracle
that would be! That's what people want – signs and
wonders. They'd flock to follow you!'

Yes, it was true. Many Jews believed that the Savior
would come floating down to earth on the clouds of
heaven. What a wonder it would be, floating down
unharmed from the topmost pinnacle of the Temple of
God. A miracle like that would convince everyone that
he was the Savior.

Again Jesus answered Satan with words from the
holy writings:

'Do not put God to the test.'

He would not seek signs from heaven to win men to

him. Miracles would not change men's hearts. Wonders would not fill them with love. That was not God's way, either.

Rule the world!

The last temptation was the worst of all. Jesus, in his mind, saw himself standing with Satan on the topmost peak of a high mountain. The kingdoms of the world, in all their glory, were spread out at his feet. And Satan said, 'I will give you all these kingdoms if you will fall down and worship me.'

Jesus knew what Satan meant. The Jews had often been conquered, in their long history. Now it was the Romans who lorded it over them. How they longed to be free! How they longed for a Savior who would lead them to victory over their enemies! A warrior Savior would win them a kingdom – even an empire! Then the kingdoms of the world would become the great kingdom of God!

Jesus knew that his work was to set up the kingdom of God on earth. How he longed for it to grow in the kingdoms of men! But would war bring peace? Would bloodshed bring loving kindness? Would hate bring love?

No, that was the way of Satan, the way of evil.

Again Jesus answered Satan in words from the holy writings:

'Go away, Satan! It is written, "Worship God, and serve him only." I will follow my Father's way.'

Then Satan knew that he was defeated, and slunk away. And the angels of God came to minister to Jesus.

The way of love

Now Jesus had rejected all the easy ways of winning men to God. Then what kind of Savior would he be?

In the writings of the prophet Isaiah, in the Bible of the Jews, there is a strange picture of the promised Savior. He would seek to win men to God by love alone. Then the kingdom of God would grow in their hearts – his kingdom of peace, and goodness, and love.

This was the hardest way of all. For it would not be easy to win men to the way of love. The Savior would be unpopular, not giving people what they wanted. He would suffer at the hands of men. He would be cast out, and done to death. But he would show men the love of God in his living and in his dying. And God would raise him up into glory.

It was hard for people to understand this kind of Savior. But this was the way Jesus chose – the way of his Father. He had decided once and for all. There was no turning back. Now he knew the way ahead.

Jesus came back from the wilderness strong and sure. Now he was ready to begin his Father's work.

Jesus chooses helpers

WHEN JESUS CAME BACK from the wilderness he naturally went to Nazareth, his home town, to begin his work for God. There, on the sabbath day, he went to the service in the synagogue, as he always had. For this was his own synagogue where he had been to school as a boy, and to worship as a man. During the service there were two readings from the holy writings, the first from a Book of Law, the second from a Book of the Prophets. Jesus was invited to read the second lesson, and to speak about it. The attendant gave him the scroll of the prophet Isaiah. He chose three verses from it which foretold the coming of God's kingdom, and read them aloud. Then he handed the scroll back and sat down to speak.

'Today these words are fulfilled,' Jesus began. 'God has filled me with his Spirit. He has sent me to proclaim the Good News that his kingdom has come.'

At first the townsfolk of Nazareth were awed by the fine words of Jesus. Then they began to realize what he was saying.

'Isn't this Jesus the carpenter?' they muttered to each other. 'Who does he think he is? We've known him since he was a boy. Why, he made and mended our tools for us!'

They began to murmur, and grew angry.

'No prophet is welcomed by his own people,' Jesus said above the hubbub. 'No prophets ever were.'

He got no further. The service should have ended with a blessing – but that day it ended in a riot. The men of Nazareth crowded around Jesus as he went out, shouting and waving their fists at him. They followed him to the hill he knew so well, till he disappeared into the caves.

Twelve apostles

Jesus left his home town and never went back to Nazareth. He began to go through villages and towns of Galilee, proclaiming the Good News. Soon he had gathered disciples – followers who believed in him. From them he chose twelve to be his apostles, that is, messengers. They would be his helpers, always with him. God's kingdom would begin with them. Then they could be sent out as messengers, spreading the Good News.

Why did Jesus choose the number twelve? The Jewish people had come from twelve tribes. So the Patriarchs, the founders of the twelve tribes, had been founders of the people of God. The twelve apostles were to be the founders of the new people of God, those who entered into his kingdom.

What kind of people would Jesus choose to be his apostles? Would they need to be clever, or holy, or important, or fine speakers?

Fishermen of Galilee

The first four men he chose were fishermen of the Sea of Galilee. It is really an inland lake, but it was always called a sea because it is so large – 12 miles long and nearly 8 miles wide. One of its names meant 'shaped like a harp'.

In its warm waters there are fourteen different kinds of fish – like carp, perch, bream, and the small St Peter's fish, still popular today. There were twelve towns, and many more villages, dotted round its shores. Their names showed how their people earned a living – names like Dried Fishes, Pickle Town, House of Fishers. Fish from the Sea of Galilee were eaten all over the land of Israel. Salted fish were sent to lands as far away as Spain, and they were a popular dish in the great city of Rome.

Jesus had grown up at Nazareth, 24 miles from the Sea of Galilee. He knew its fishermen well – strong, burly men, bronzed by the sun. He may have helped to build their boats – small, sturdy craft, each with one sail, and with room for six men. Sometimes they fished with a harpoon, either from the shore or from a boat. At night they would use a torch to attract the fish. Sometimes a fisherman stood on the shore, casting a hook and line. At other times he would use a weighted hand-net, whirling it round, and flinging it into the water in the shape of a cone, where its weights sank it and the fish were caught inside it.

Most fish were caught by fishermen who clubbed together to buy their own boat and nets. They worked as a group of six men, with one as leader, and shared the money from the sale of their fish. They worked with large drag-nets, letting them down into the water, drawing the ends together in a circle, and then pulling the nets into the boat, trapping all the fish inside. After fishing, the precious nets had to be hung up for drying, and cleaning, and mending.

One day Jesus came to the Sea of Galilee. He saw the brothers named Andrew and Simon in their boat, some way off shore, casting their drag-net. When they heard Jesus calling they pulled in the net, and turned their boat toward the shore. Soon it was scraping on the sand.

'Come!' Jesus said to Andrew and Simon. 'Follow me. You are fishermen. I will make you fishers of men.'

Already the two brothers knew Jesus well. Andrew had been a disciple of John the Baptist, and he had brought his brother Simon to Jesus. Already they believed in Jesus, and would gladly give their lives to him.

At the call of Jesus they left their boat and nets and followed him. They knew what he meant, and what their work would be. Just as they gathered fish into their nets, so they would gather men into the kingdom of God.

Jesus walked on toward another boat, further on. It belonged to old Zebedee, a well-to-do fisherman. James and John, his two sturdy sons, were sitting in the boat with him and his hired men, mending their nets. Jesus called out to them, 'James! John! Come! Follow me.'

And they, too, left everything and followed the prophet whom they had come to love.

Jesus knew the men he had chosen – strong in body and spirit. He gave Simon a new name – Peter, which means Rock. He gave a fine nickname to James and John, who were fiery young men – Sons of Thunder, he called them.

The four fishermen knew each other well. For they fished as a team, with Peter, a born leader, in charge. Peter and James and John seem to have understood Jesus best of all the apostles. For they were the closest to him, and he always chose them to be with him.

The tax-collector of Capernaum
Simon Peter lived at Capernaum, a busy port on the northwest shore of the lake. The Romans had a garrison

there, for their main highway from north to south ran through the town. Capernaum had something else, as an **important road center. It had its own customs-house,** where both fishermen and travellers had to pay Roman taxes. There sat the tax-gatherer, Matthew Levi, with a Roman soldier standing by in case of trouble. For people hated paying Roman taxes, as well as their own Jewish taxes. They turned their hate on the tax-gatherers, Jews who collected taxes for the Romans. They were traitors to their own people – and everyone knew how they became rich by charging higher taxes than they should.

So Matthew Levi was hated and despised, rich in money but poor in friends. How astonished he was, one day, when a shadow fell over his counting-table and he looked up to see Jesus. What on earth could the popular prophet want with him, a despised tax-gatherer?

'Come, Matthew,' Jesus said. 'Follow me.'

The prophet really wanted him! Matthew jumped up eagerly. He was so excited that he left everything, just as it was, and followed Jesus.

Then Matthew prepared a great feast at his house in honor of the prophet. He invited all his friends to meet Jesus. Most of them, of course, were tax-gatherers, and other despised men. The good people of Capernaum were shocked to see the prophet in such shameful company.

'Why do you sit at table with such evil men?' they said in disgust.

'Only sick people need a doctor,' Jesus answered them. 'I have not come to call people like you, so sure that you are right with God. I have come to call those who are sinners, but whose hearts are open to God.'

Twelve different men

Tax-collectors like Matthew were traitors to the Jews. Men called Zealots were just the opposite. They were fierce patriots who fought ceaselessly against the Romans. Jesus chose a Zealot named Simon to be one of his apostles.

Philip, another apostle, had been brought to Jesus by Andrew, and they were close friends. Philip, in turn, brought his friend called Bartholomew, and sometimes Nathaniel. Others whom Jesus chose to be apostles were Jude, Thomas, and another James, called James the Younger to distinguish him from the brother of John.

Now these eleven apostles were different in many ways. But all of them were men of Galilee, in the north of Israel. The twelfth apostle was Judas, called Iscariot – for he came from Kerioth, a village of Judaea, in the south of Israel. So he was the odd man out. But all the twelve, however different, were united by their faith in Jesus.

Jesus the popular prophet

Capernaum was a fine center for the work of Jesus. When he was there he stayed at Simon Peter's house. From Capernaum he went out, with the twelve, to towns and villages of Galilee. Everywhere he spread the Good News of God and his love. He showed God's love in all he did. He loved everyone, and despised no one. He spoke with authority, as if God spoke through him. His teaching was easy to understand, too. For he taught in fine, everyday stories from life around him. The love of God was seen, too, in his caring for those who were sick in mind or in body.

So the crowds thronged around the popular prophet. All day long the power of God's love flowed out of Jesus. He hated evil, but he loved evil-doers. For he loved most those who most needed love. The kingdom of God was at work in him.

So Jesus sowed the seed of the kingdom in the hearts of men, and trained the twelve apostles so that they would be messengers of the kingdom.

The loving father

ARMER BOAZ WAS A HAPPY MAN who had
worked hard all his life, and now he owned a
fine farm. He had been blessed with two sons
whom he loved dearly. Now he looked
forward to the time when he would have
grandchildren. For they would gladden his old age, and
preserve his name among men. How content he was, as
he looked out over his cornfields, his sheep and cattle,
his orchards and vineyards.

But his happiness was not to last. Simon, his elder
son, was a true countryman, spending long days in the
fields, quite content to be a farmer. But Jason, his
younger son, was quite different. He was bored with the
dull life on the farm, where nothing ever happened. He
had heard of grand cities across the river Jordan, full of
excitement and pleasure and fun. How he longed to get
away from the dreary farm, and to see the world.

'Besides,' he said to himself, 'Simon will inherit the
farm, as the eldest son. That's the law, so that the family
will go on through him. I'm the younger son – so I've got
to make my own way in the world.'

Jason grew more and more restless. 'I'm a man now,'
he thought to himself, '17 years old. It's time I left home.
I know what I'll do. The law says that the eldest son
must inherit two-thirds of his father's wealth. So as I'm

the only other son I shall get the other third for myself, sooner or later. I'll claim it now! Yes, that's it! I'll travel abroad and go into business. I'll soon show them how clever I am!'

He went straight to his father.

'Father, I want my share of your estate. I'd like it now so that I can travel, and make my own living. I'll do well, you'll see.'

Farmer Boaz was saddened by his son's rude demand. But he did not answer him sternly. Nor did he stand in Jason's way. He must be free to become himself. So Farmer Boaz sold off some of his animals, and part of his land, to raise one third of the value of his estate.

Jason could not wait to be off, striding eagerly down the road with the bag of silver. Farmer Boaz watched him go with sorrow in his heart and tears in his eyes, till his dear son disappeared into the distance.

The rich young man at Jerash

How excited Jason was when he reached Jerash, the city of his dreams, on the other side of the river Jordan. Still today its ruins show what a wonderful city it was, built by the Greeks, and made even more magnificent by the Romans.

Jason had the sense to put his silver with the bankers. Now he could get money from them whenever he wished, with interest added to it. He was soon entering into the exciting life of the town. There were splendid shops where he bought fine new clothes. At the hippodrome there were all the thrills of the horse races. At the stadium he watched the skilful Greek athletes **competing in their sports and games.** At the theater there was a new play every week. And every day, as the custom was, Jason lounged at the public baths with his friends.

For of course the rich young Jew was soon popular. He made merry with his new-found friends, with music and dancing, feasting and drinking. 'Now I'm really living!' Jason said to himself happily.

Many of the finest buildings in Jerash were temples of the gods and goddesses of the Greeks and the Romans. Jason had been brought up to worship the one true God of the Jews, and to live strictly by his sacred laws. He had been taught that these gods and goddesses were nothing but heathen idols, and that these people were nothing but foolish pagans. How glad Jason was to have got away from all that! Why, now that he was wearing Greek clothes and following Greek customs, he was quite at home with his new friends – he felt he was one of them.

Jason had no time to think about going into business

31

and making money. Anyway there was no need to worry
– he could always get money from the bankers. But the
day came when they had bad news for Jason. All his
money was spent.

At once Jason thought of his friends. 'No need to
worry,' he said to himself. 'My friends will look after me,
after all I've done for them.' But he soon discovered that
they were fair-weather friends. His father's money had
bought their friendship. Now that the money was gone
they were gone too. Now he was alone – a penniless
stranger in a strange land.

The beggar with the pigs

Jason tried to find a job to earn money for food. But
there were no jobs to be had in the town. Times were
hard, and there was a great famine in the land.

He went out into the countryside. After all, he knew
a lot about farming – he'd soon get a job on the land. He
tried one farm after another. No one wanted the ragged
beggar. Then a pig-farmer took pity on him, and gave
him a job as a swineherd, looking after the pigs. It was
the lowest job of all. But Jason was too hungry to be
proud.

There was something else about his lowly job. Greeks
and Romans were fond of pig's meat. They used pigs as
sacrifices to their gods, too. That was why pigs were
'unclean' in Jewish law – Jews must have nothing to do
with them. So Jason had to go against his religion to
keep alive. But at least he had food – the rough honey-
beans from the carob tree, used to fatten up the pigs for
market. There was no other food for a penniless beggar.

Jason had plenty of time to think, as he sat in his
filthy rags watching the pigs. He began to come to his
senses. 'What a fool I've been,' he said to himself. 'I was
much better off at home. I had everything I needed on
the farm. I was respected by all the servants as one of
the family. Look at me now! Why, even my father's
servants are much better off than I am. I have no food,
no money, no clothes, no shelter, no friends.'

Then he decided. 'I'll go back home. Yes, that's it. I'll
go back to my father. I'll own up that I've sinned against
God. I'll admit that I've been a bad son, not respecting
him, not obeying him. I've had my share of his estate
and lost it – I know that. I can't expect him to take me
back as his son – or even as a family servant. I'll ask
him to let me be one of the hired laborers on his farm.
I'll say to him, "I'm not fit to be treated as your son. But
please take me on as just a worker in the fields." '

A father's love

It was a long, hard journey back home, hobbling along
stony roads, eating any scraps or berries he could find,

sleeping by the roadside. No one could have recognized the dirty, tattered beggar as the proud son of Farmer Boaz.

But someone did. Farmer Boaz had been sad and unhappy ever since Jason had gone away. Every day he went up on the flat roof of his house, gazing into the distance, watching, waiting, longing. It was he who recognized the beggar hobbling in the distance. At last! His dear, dear son!

Farmer Boaz hurried down the stairway from the roof, and ran down the road, forgetting all about his dignity. He clasped his son in his arms, crying aloud with joy. Jason could hardly speak as his father hugged and kissed him. When he could, he began the speech he had planned: 'Father, I've sinned against heaven and against you. I'm not fit to be called your son. Please take me on as one of your hired laborers.'

His father didn't hear a word. He was busy clapping his hands, calling for his servants. 'My son has come back!' he cried to them, as they came running out. 'Quick! Fetch my best robe to honor him as my son! Bring one of my rings for his finger, to give him my authority! Bring slippers too – we can't have him going barefoot like a servant!

'Kill the fatted calf!' he called to others. 'Prepare a feast! We must eat and drink and be merry. For my son was dead – and now he's alive again! He was lost – and now he's found!'

A brother's hatred

What a feast it was! And what merry-making! There was
the music of flutes and pipes, drums and tambourines,
with everyone joining in the round dance. There was
singing, stamping of feet, clapping of hands. What a din
they made! Anyone could have heard it a long way off.

Someone did. It was Simon, the elder son of Farmer
Boaz, trudging wearily back home after a long day in the
fields. He called a servant. 'What's all the fuss? What's
the singing and dancing and shouting for?' The servant
told him that his brother had come back, safe and sound,
and that his delighted father had ordered a feast. Simon
was furious when he heard the news.

The servant hurried to tell Farmer Boaz that Simon
was coming back from the fields. 'Then run to him
quickly! Ask him to join us and take his place of honour
at the feast!' said Farmer Boaz.

'What!' shouted Simon to the servant when he came
back. 'Does he think I'm going to make merry in honor
of that good-for-nothing, just because the lazy rascal's
come back? I'm certainly not going in – and you can tell
him so!'

Then Farmer Boaz himself came out to plead with his
elder son. He began to speak kind and loving words. But
Simon cut him short, in his rage. He shouted in his
anger, 'All these years I've slaved on your farm! I've

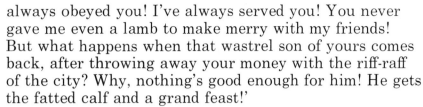

always obeyed you! I've always served you! You never gave me even a lamb to make merry with my friends! But what happens when that wastrel son of yours comes back, after throwing away your money with the riff-raff of the city? Why, nothing's good enough for him! He gets the fatted calf and a grand feast!'

Farmer Boaz loved Simon just as much as he loved Jason. He understood just how Simon felt, and why he was so angry. He did not speak sternly at such rudeness. He did not mention that Simon had done no more than his duty as a son. He did not mention that the whole estate now came to Simon, so that he was really working for himself. He did not mention that Simon could have a feast any time he wanted.

Nor did he complain at Simon's hard and bitter heart. He knew that if Simon had been in his place he would have turned Jason away and rejected him, as the law permitted. So would most fathers.

But Farmer Boaz was not like other fathers. The love in his heart was like the love of the heavenly Father for all his children.

'Simon, my son, my dear son,' he said gently. 'You are always with me – I know that I can always rely on you. All that I have is yours. Jason is my son just as you are. I love you both dearly. It makes me so happy to have you both with me.

'It was only right to make merry, and rejoice, and be glad. I was afraid I would never see Jason again, when he went away. He was dead – and now he's alive again. He was lost – and now he is found.

'Come in with me, my son. Come and share my joy, and make my happiness complete.'

God the loving father

We feel for Simon, the elder son, in this story. We sympathize with him, not with Jason. And that shows how different our love is from the love of God.

For this story is one of the parables of Jesus. A parable puts two things side by side, likens them to each other, and compares them, so that we can learn from it.

The loving father of this story is like God. Some of his children are like Jason. They are selfish, greedy, and foolish, and go their own way. Others are like Simon. They seem so good, so obedient, so loyal. But in their hard hearts there is no room for love, or sympathy, or forgiveness. Simon was no closer to his father than Jason, even if he did stay at home.

Jesus used parables like this to teach the Good News of God and his kingdom. The father's love embraced both his children equally. That is what the heavenly Father is like. His endless love embraces all his children.

The good shepherd

JACOB LIVED IN ONE OF THE LITTLE VILLAGES which nestled among the hills of Galilee. He had worked hard all his life. Now he owned his own white-washed house, where he lived with his wife and children, and a plot of land for growing crops to feed his family. Jacob's greatest joy was his flock of sheep, out on the hills. He had been a shepherd boy, and he had always wanted a flock of his own. He had started with a few, and now he had a full hundred sheep. The well-watered hills of Galilee gave lush green grass for sheep to grow fat. But it was only on a very special occasion that a sheep was killed to make a feast.

Sheep were kept for milk and, most of all, for wool. Miriam, the wife of Jacob, spun the wool on her spindle, and made cloth with it on her loom. From her cloth she made warm clothes for the family – especially the cloaks which kept out the fierce heat of day and the bitter cold of night.

Jacob loved, best of all, to be with the sheep. But now Benjamin, his eldest son, was old enough to go shepherding alone. Jacob had long been training him to become a good shepherd. The other children liked to help, too. For since the family kept the same sheep for a long time they became real pets, each with its own name.

The sheep knew their names, and the voices of the family, too. That was why they came so quickly when they were called. Every sheep was precious, not just for milk and wool, but because each one was a friend of the family.

Good shepherds and bad shepherds

Benjamin was proud to carry his shepherd's crook, a staff with a curved end to fit under a sheep, even if it was taller than he was. He was determined to become a good shepherd, caring for his flock, not for himself. He knew it was a hard life, out in all weathers. The good shepherd was with his flock all the time, watching over them, finding pasture and water for them, guarding them from danger. A sheep could easily slip and fall on the rocky slopes, and get trapped. There were cruel thorns, poisonous snakes, and always beasts of prey. When night came on the sheep had to be made secure inside the fold, with the shepherd to guard them by night as by day.

There were bad shepherds. They were hired by rich men to look after their big flocks. But hired men cared for the money, not for the sheep. When a wolf came after the flock they fled to safety, caring for themselves and not for the flock. Nor did they worry if a sheep was lost. What did one matter, when all the rest were safe? Benjamin was horrified by stories of hired shepherds like these.

A lost sheep

One evening Benjamin was leading his flock to the fold, just as usual. It had been a happy day. In the morning he had found good pasture. Toward noon he led the sheep to water – still, calm water, for they were frightened by swift-running water. There they had rested during the heat of the day, with the shade of trees. There Benjamin had his dinner, which his mother had packed in the skin bag that he slung over his shoulder, and he drank water from the leather bottle tied to his waist.

After dinner he had practised with his sling, made from a piece of goat skin and two leather strings. His target was a stone he had set upright, some distance away. There were plenty of pebbles by the water. The wide center part of the skin was hollowed out to take a small round stone. Benjamin put a pebble in the hollow, twirled the sling round his head, let one string go, and the pebble flew to its target. He was getting more hits every day, but he wanted to be sure of hitting every time. He must be able to drop a pebble exactly in front of a wandering sheep, to turn it back to the flock – and to hit first time any wild beast threatening the sheep.

Now it was evening, and the fold was in sight. Two other shepherds from the village were already there, so

Benjamin would have company for the night. There was plenty of room for all three flocks in the big fold. Its high stone walls had thorn bushes piled on top, to make them higher still and keep out the beasts of prey – hyenas, jackals, and wolves. The only way they could get at the sheep was through the entrance to the fold. But the shepherd, wrapped in his thick cloak, lay across the opening. He himself was the door. He guarded his sheep with his own life.

When he reached the fold Benjamin held his crook over the opening, so that the sheep could only enter one at a time. Now he could count them, one by one, as a good shepherd always did, to make sure that none was missing. There should have been one hundred. But that night there were ninety-nine. There was no doubt about it – one of the flock was missing. It must have strayed and wandered off. Now it was lost, and in great danger.

There was not a moment to lose. Leaving the rest of the flock safely in the fold, guarded by the two shepherds, Benjamin ran down the hill towards the village. His lungs were bursting by the time he reached his house and hammered on the door.

'Father! Father! One of the sheep is missing.'

Finding a lost sheep

Jacob quickly reached for his cloak. He grabbed his horn, filled with soothing oil for cuts and bruises, and tucked it into his belt. He took up his rod, a club made from the tough root of a tree and studded with bits of metal, and tied its strap around his wrist. Then, seizing his crook, he was ready, and father and son set off into the dark and danger of the bitter night.

They made first for the fold, and then began to retrace the way that Benjamin had led the flock during the day. Benjamin felt so proud to be with his father on this dangerous adventure. Jacob, too, was proud of his son, growing up to be a good shepherd. But, of course, neither of them spoke a word. For both were listening keenly, waiting for the tiny bleat of a lamb. They heard rustlings, and the sounds of night animals on the prowl. Benjamin led the way, with his crook ready for any attack, and his father followed, keeping his rod firmly in his grasp.

Benjamin's keen young ears were first to pick out the sound they had been longing for. Eagerly he hurried towards it, his father close behind, till at last he could hear it close to him. He stood near the edge of a precipice – and the bleating came from below. Father and son lay down and crawled to the edge till they could see over. There, held fast on a ledge below, was the precious lamb, bleating helplessly. It was caught in a thick bush – but only that had saved it from being dashed to death on the rocks far below.

Benjamin murmured comforting words to the lamb as his father stretched his crook down toward the bush. He carefully pushed aside the branches holding the lamb fast. Then he put the curve of his crook under it, and began to lift it slowly up to him, till he could reach it with his hand. Holding the trembling lamb to his chest, he slowly moved his body back from the edge of the precipice. Then he passed it to Benjamin who fondled it in his arms. It was shivering with fear as it nestled against him, nuzzling his face.

Jacob took the stopper out of his horn of oil, and now they went over the lamb's body, picking out thorns and bits of twigs, and soothing cuts with oil. Benjamin tucked the lamb inside his cloak, close to his chest, warm and safe. Now they were ready for the journey home.

They still had to be on guard as they went through the night. But now they could talk – and share their joy that the precious lamb had been found safe and well.

The joy of finding the lost

It was far into the night as they came down the hillside toward the village below. But they could see plenty of lights. Friends and neighbors had heard the news, and they were waiting anxiously – for the night was full of dangers.

How delighted they were to hear the happy voice of Jacob, shouting aloud as he came into the village. They rushed to unbar their doors and ran out to greet him and Benjamin.

'I've found it! I've found my lamb!' shouted Jacob. 'Come to my house! Come and share my joy!'

What a happy party they had that night! Miriam hurried to set out food and wine for the unexpected guests. They used up everything in the house – but what did that matter? They were all so happy, sharing in Jacob's joy.

And while everyone was making merry, Miriam was thinking about her husband.

'What a good shepherd Jacob is!' she thought to herself. 'Why, he's more full of joy over finding one lost lamb than over all the other ninety-nine sheep who are safe in the fold!'

God the good shepherd

Jesus told this parable to devout men of religion – Scribes, who were scholars of the law of God, and Pharisees who lived strictly by it. They were criticizing him for mixing with people they despised – tax-gatherers and the like. How could a true prophet mix with such

40

sinners? After telling his story Jesus said, 'It is just like that with God, the heavenly Father. He loves every one of his children, like Jacob loving every one of his sheep. He knows and cares for each one, and cannot rest if one of them is lost. I tell you, there is more joy in heaven over one lost sinner who comes back to God than over ninety-nine devout men who are safe in the fold.'

Jesus had never forgotten the days and nights he had spent with shepherds, when he was a boy. He knew good shepherds and bad shepherds. He spoke of himself as a shepherd: 'I am the good shepherd. I know my sheep, and they know me. They follow when I call, and I lead them. The hired shepherd runs away when he sees the wolf coming. I never leave my sheep. I am their guide, and their guard. I am the door of the fold, and I am ready to lay down my life for my sheep.'

The Kingdom of God

ESUS HAD GROWN UP in the countryside of Galilee. He knew the work of the farmer, just as he knew the ways of fishermen and shepherds. Many of the people of Galilee worked on the land. So making parables from their daily work was a fine way of teaching about the kingdom of God. There was another reason why Jesus drew parables from nature. He saw God at work in nature – his beauty in wild flowers, his care in providing for the birds of the air. God had made laws for nature, just as he had made laws for men. So a story from nature was a simple parable of the kingdom of God.

When a farmer has sown his corn, said Jesus, there is nothing more that he can do. The seed grows mysteriously, of its own accord. It grows secretly, by the laws which God has made for it. It grows slowly – first the blade, then the ear, then the grain in the ear. The farmer can do nothing to hasten the harvest, for there are no short cuts in nature. He must be patient. He must have faith. He has sown the seed and harvest will come.

The kingdom of God is like that, said Jesus. It is not like an earthly kingdom. It is the rule of God in the hearts of men. Jesus and his apostles, like the prophets of old, were sowing the seed. It would grow mysteriously,

43

secretly, slowly, according to God's laws. The disciples
must have faith that the seed would grow, and the
harvest come, in the hearts of men.

The mustard seed

At first, Jesus was a popular prophet among the people
of Galilee. But as time went on there was growing
opposition to him, especially among the religious leaders
of the people. Pharisees were the most devout people of
all, for they lived strictly by the sacred laws. Jesus
angered them by his new teaching, and by his criticism
of them. They warned the people against Jesus. His
disciples began to lose heart. People did not flock to join
them, and they were still few. How could the kingdom of
God grow from such small beginnings?

Jesus told a parable to help them understand. It was
about black mustard, so common in the land of Israel. Its
seed was so tiny that people made a saying from it.
Anything very small was said to be 'like a grain of
mustard seed'. But people also knew how the mustard
seed could grow. It could be simply a plant, with bright
yellow flowers, or a thick bush. It could also grow into
the size of a tree, eleven and a half feet high, with thick
branches spreading far and wide, and birds sheltering in
them.

The kingdom of God is just like that mustard seed,
said Jesus to his disciples. From the tiniest of seeds
would grow a great tree, so that birds from near and far
could find shelter in its branches. From the tiny group of
disciples would grow the great kingdom of God, so that
men of all nations could find shelter within it.

The sower

But Jesus knew well that not all the seed sown in the
ground grew up and gave a harvest. Everything
depended on the soil in which it grew. He spoke of this
in a parable of the sower. He told it to answer another
question of the disciples: why do so few of those who
hear the Good News take the seed into their hearts and
bear a harvest?

The farmer in Galilee sowed his seed after the early
rains of autumn. Today we plough the land and then sow
the seed – a farmer then did just the opposite, and sowed
the seed first. He carried the seed in a basket, or in a
fold of his tunic, and threw it over the earth, a handful
at a time. It fell everywhere – on the path beside the
field, trodden by the villagers; on stony ground; among
thorns; and on good ground. This was quite deliberate,
for the farmer was going to plough up the whole field,
including the path and the thorn bushes. His plough,
pulled by oxen or asses, pushed the seed into the furrow.

Jesus did not explain his parables. He wanted people

44

to think for themselves, to decide what they meant, and to act upon them. The first Christians often told these parables in their own teaching. They added to the parable of Jesus exactly what they thought each detail meant. This is the explanation they added to the parable of the sower.

Some of the seed fell on the path that had been trodden hard by villagers and baked hard by the sun. The birds had a free meal even before the farmer arrived with his plough. In the same way, some people hear the word of God – but at once the spirit of evil enters, and snatches away the seed before it has any time to take root.

Some of the seed fell on stony, rocky ground. Only a thin layer of earth covered the limestone rock beneath. The shallow soil was not deep enough for roots to grow. The seed sprouted quickly, and sprang up. But without roots and moisture it was quickly scorched by the sun, and withered away. There are people without roots, too. They hear the Good News with joy, but their enthusiasm quickly fades. As soon as any trouble comes they give it up, and fall away.

Some of the seed fell among thorns. But the thorns grew quicker and stronger, and soon choked it. There are many thorns in the hearts of men. Poor people are choked with worries about getting work and food and clothes and homes. Rich men are choked with worries about keeping their treasure safe from thieves, getting good profits in their trading, getting good harvests on their land. How hard it was for a rich man to enter into the kingdom of God, said Jesus.

Some of the seed fell on good ground, soil that was rich and fertile, ready to receive the seed when the plough turned it in. It bore a good harvest, more than making up for the wasted seed, as the farmer knew it would. A ten-fold return on the seed he had sown was a good return for a farmer in Galilee. But in the parable of Jesus the return was thirty-fold, sixty-fold, even one hundred-fold! This was wonderful – but this was God at work.

The harvest of the kingdom would be just as bountiful, said Jesus. The disciples should not worry Over seed that took no root, and labor that seemed in vain. The kingdom of God would bear a rich harvest in hearts that were ready to receive the seed.

Finding treasure

What kind of people were ready to receive the kingdom of God? Some found it quite by accident.

It was like that with a man taking a walk in the countryside. As he was crossing an abandoned field he stumbled against something hard, sticking out of the ground. Curious to find out what it was, he got down and scraped away the earth. Imagine his delight when he uncovered a strong box – and inside it was buried treasure!

In ancient times it was a common custom to bury precious things in the earth. It was safe there from thieves, and from soldiers in time of war. For no one else knew where it was. The proverb said: The safest place for money is the earth. But a man might bury his treasure, go on a journey, and never return – he might die in a distant place. The law said that if someone found a buried treasure like this in land that he owned he could keep that treasure.

No wonder that the man hastily covered up the treasure-chest, and hurried into town to buy that field. The price was high – much more money than he had. But he sold everything he possessed to raise it: his house, his furniture, his clothes, his ox, his ass, his goat – everything. Now he had enough money to buy the field. Now the precious treasure was his.

The treasure, in that parable of Jesus, is the kingdom of God. A man may come across the kingdom of God by accident. But when he has found it he knows how precious it is. He gives up everything to win it. For he knows it is the greatest treasure of all.

Finding a precious pearl

Other people only found the kingdom of God by searching for it everywhere.

It was like that with a rich merchant who traded in pearls. He loved them for their beauty, as well as for their value. He travelled far and wide, always searching for finer pearls. One day, on his travels, he found the most exquisite pearl he had ever seen. 'I must have it!' he said to himself. 'I can't live without it.' The owner promised to keep it for him, till he had raised the huge price. The merchant hurried back home, sold his fine house, his lands, and all his beloved pearls. It was more than worth it to win that wonderful pearl.

People like this do not stumble across the kingdom of God by chance. They have to search hard for it. But when they find it they know that it is worth more than all they possess. The kingdom of God is costly. It may demand everything a man possesses to win it. But he knows it is the finest treasure of all.

Treasure in heaven

The parables of Jesus are often called 'earthly stories with a heavenly meaning'. In these parables Jesus was comparing earthly treasure with heavenly treasure. He also said, 'Don't store up treasure on earth. You know it won't last. Fine metal is ruined by rust. Fine clothes are eaten away by moths. Thieves break in and steal.

'Lay up a heavenly treasure. Store precious things in your hearts. Be rich toward God. No one can take that kind of treasure from you. Nothing can spoil it.

'Where your treasure is there will your heart be also.'

The goodness of God

IN A HOT COUNTRY, like the land of Israel, drink is a matter of life and death. Water was scarce and precious in the time of Jesus. There was plenty of rain, but it came in a few days of violent storms. Much of the water was wasted, for there were no reservoirs. Country folk depended on wells, and springs, and streams. In the towns water-sellers went round the streets, carrying their water in bags made of sewn-up skins.

Most families had milk to drink from their goats and sheep. But the favorite and most common drink was red wine, made from grapes. Vines grew plentifully, and there were vineyards everywhere. Each vineyard had its wine-press for squeezing the juice from the grapes. It also had its watch-tower, for guarding the vines from jackals and little foxes, as well as from thieves. Grape-harvest lasted from August to September. At the end of September the rainy season began, and all the grapes had to be gathered in before the rains started. Every day, every hour, mattered to get the grapes picked in time. The owner of a big vineyard needed every man he could get to gather grapes before it was too late. It was like that with Farmer Jacob.

Workers in the vineyard

Jacob had a fine, large vineyard, and a bumper havest of

48

grapes to be gathered in. All his servants had been working for days, and picking was going well. But time was getting short. He simply had to hire more workers.

So Jacob went out to the market-place at dawn, about 6 o'clock, when the working day began. Already the best workers were gathered there, waiting to bargain for the best pay they could get. Jacob offered them a denarius, a common silver coin of the Romans, used in Israel. It was **a good day's wage for a laborer, and the men went off** cheerfully to begin a long day's work in Jacob's vineyard.

Still Jacob was not satisfied. It was getting urgent now – every hour mattered. He went out again at 9 o'clock, in case there were any other men wanting work, and found some idling there.

'Go and work in my vineyard,' he said. 'I'll pay you a fair wage.'

The men trusted Jacob and set off for the vineyard. They were glad to get work, for times were hard, and many men were unemployed.

Jacob went out again at noon, and at 3 o'clock in the afternoon. Still he found men with nothing to do. He made the same promise to them, and they too went to work in his vineyard, trusting him to pay a fair wage for their work.

Jacob even hurried back to the market-place at 5 o'clock, when there was only one hour left of the working day. But it was a race against time, now, to finish harvesting the grapes. There were still men there, idling and gossiping together.

'Why do you lounge around here all day, doing nothing?' he chided them.

'We can't get work. No one will hire us,' they said.

'Well I'll hire you,' said Jacob. 'Hurry into my vineyard and get to work. There's still an hour of daylight left.'

Off they went, relying only on Jacob's generosity.

Paying the workers

When dusk came on, and work ended for the day, it was time for Jacob's steward to pay the laborers.

'Give all of them a full day's wage,' Jacob ordered. 'Start with those I took on last of all.'

Imagine the delight of those laborers taken on last. Each of them received a silver denarius, a full day's wage, for only one hour's work! How generous Farmer Jacob had been to them!

Then came the workers hired during the day. Each of them was given a denarius, too. They had trusted Jacob to pay what was fair. A full day's wage was much more than they had dared to hope for.

Last of all came the men who had done a full day's work. They had seen the others paid so handsomely that they quite expected Jacob to be generous to them too. But each of them got exactly what he had bargained for – one silver denarius.

They began to murmur among themselves. They grumbled openly and soon worked themselves up. They shook their fists angrily in the direction of Jacob's house. They even went up to the house, dragging the other workers with them.

Jacob came out, and the ring-leader shouted at him rudely, 'We've slaved for twelve hours in your vineyard – all through the heat of the day!' he cried. 'These layabouts have only worked for one hour – in the cool of the evening! Yet you've paid us no more than them!'

Jacob answered him courteously. 'My dear sir, you seem to think I've cheated you. But I'm doing you no wrong. Didn't you bargain with me for a silver denarius for the day's work? I have kept my bargain, haven't I?

'As for the other workers, I decided to pay them a denarius too. Are you complaining about my generosity? Can't I do what I like with my own money? If I choose to pay these men the same as you that's my business – not yours. Are you envious, just because I am generous? You've got what you bargained for. Take your wages, and be off with you.'

Men in God's vineyard

What a topsy-turvy story that was! Like many of the parables of Jesus it turned everything upside down. No one would make money, running a vineyard like that. No employer could run a business like that.

But this parable was not a lesson in running a business and making money. It was teaching about God and his generosity.

Jacob was a generous man. He knew that unemployed men had hungry wives and children. In fact their needs were greater than those of good workers who got regular work. It was not their fault that they were unemployed. Jacob decided to make this clear to the other workers by deliberately paying first the men taken on last. If he had paid first those who had worked a full day they would have gone home quite happy. They would not have known about Jacob's generosity to the others. There would have been no trouble.

Jacob was like the heavenly Father, and the workers were like different kinds of men.

Some men thought that they could bargain with God. If they kept every detail of his sacred law they must be righteous in his sight. It was as if God kept a register, and recorded all their pious deeds. When they were

added up it was obvious that God owed them a reward, for being so righteous. No wonder that they were so proud, looking down on ordinary folk. No wonder that they were so self-righteous, despising sinful men like tax-gatherers. There was no love in their religion, for God or for man. It was simply bargaining with God.

Other men were like the workers taken on during the day. They did not try to bargain with God. They simply trusted in God's goodness and justice. They had faith in him. How well rewarded they were!

Others were like the men taken on for the last hour of the day. They could not bargain. They deserved little, they expected little. How richly rewarded they were! They, more than all the others, knew the goodness and generosity of God.

Jesus told this parable to answer a question that Peter had asked: 'Lord, we have given up everything to follow you. What reward will God give us?'

The answer was plain. Do not think of rewards. Do not try to bargain with God. Trust in his goodness, his generosity, his love.

The goodness of God

Jesus used the ways of nature to show how generous God is to men. 'You remember what the old law said – "Love your neighbor and hate your enemy." But I say to you, love your enemies. Then you will be sons of your heavenly Father. For he does not pick and choose. He has no favorites. His sun ripens the crops of both good men and evil men. He sends rain to water the fields of both just men and unjust men. How generous he is!'

Jesus used the ways of people, too. 'You fathers and mothers are good to your children, aren't you? You always try to give them what they need. Suppose that your son is hungry, and asks you for a small loaf of bread to eat. Do you give him a stone? Or if he asks for a fish, do you give him a snake? No, of course you don't.

'If you then, being evil, know how to give good gifts to your children, how much more will your heavenly Father give good things to those who ask him.

'Ask him for what you need. You will find how good and generous God is.'

The forgiveness of God

NE DAY JESUS WAS INVITED to the house of a rich Pharisee named Simon who lived in Capernaum. It happened, it seems, on the sabbath, the rest day in each week, set aside to the worship of God. All good Jews went to the synagogue for the service. The congregation of men and boys sat downstairs in the synagogue. Women and girls followed the service from their gallery upstairs. Among them, that day, was a woman called Miriam. Everyone shunned her, for she was well-known as a sinner, a woman who did not live a pure life. She had only dared to come because she had heard that the new prophet, Jesus, was to speak. Already she had been told wonderful things about him and his message of God's love for sinners.

There was someone else who wanted to know more about Jesus. It was Simon, the wealthy and devout Pharisee. He was curious to find out if this Jesus was a true prophet. So were his friends among the Pharisees. Simon decided to ask Jesus to eat at his house after the service, and to invite his friends. That would give them a chance to make up their minds about the prophet. Jesus was a friend to all, rich or poor, high or low, good or bad. He accepted Simon's invitation, and came to his house after the service.

Simon did not want to honor Jesus too much – after all, he might not be a genuine prophet. So he did not bother about the strict customs for welcoming guests – washing the guest's dusty feet with water, giving him the kiss of greeting, offering perfumed oil to freshen his face and hair.

Simon led Jesus straight to the couches, grouped round low tables. Wealthy Jews followed the Greek and Roman custom of reclining at meals on couches, instead of sitting on mats. The guests lay full length on the couches, their feet stretched out behind them. So anyone coming into the room stood at their feet. The room opened on to the courtyard so that servants could come in with food, and pass among the guests. That was how Miriam was able to come in unnoticed, and to stand at the feet of Jesus.

The great love of a sinner

Miriam had been deeply moved by the words of Jesus in the synagogue. She knew that she was an outcast, according to the religion of her people, and that she had no hope of God's forgiveness. Yet Jesus had spoken of God's tender love and forgiveness for sinners. His words had completely changed her life. For now she knew that God loved her, sinner that she was, and that her sins were forgiven.

Miriam longed to show her thankfulness to the prophet. When she heard that Jesus was going to the house of Simon she hurried home to get her most priceless possession. It was a tiny alabaster flask of costly perfume. Then she came with it to the house of Simon, and crept in unnoticed among the busy servants.

When Miriam stood at the feet of Jesus she was overcome. Tears of joy and gratitude poured down her face, and fell on to his feet. She sank to her knees beside him, removed the covering from her head, and untwined her long hair. She completely forgot herself, and the terrible disgrace for a woman to let down her hair in the presence of men. With her long silken tresses she wiped away her tears from the feet of Jesus. She opened her precious flask and anointed them with the costly perfume. Then she kissed his feet – the symbol of thankfulness to one who had saved your life. For Jesus had saved her from her past. He had given her a new life.

The little love of a Pharisee

Simon had noticed Miriam and what she was doing. He knew her, and her bad reputation. He thought to himself, 'If this man was a true prophet he would know what sort of woman was touching him.'

Jesus could read Simon's thoughts.

'Simon,' he said, 'I have something to say to you.'

'What is it, Teacher?' said Simon politely.

'There were two men who each owed a debt to a money-lender. One owed him fifty pounds. The other owed him five pounds. Neither of them could repay him. He forgave both of them their debts to him. Now, which of the two men will love him more, do you think?'

'The man who was forgiven most, I suppose,' Simon replied.

'You are right,' said Jesus. Then, turning toward Miriam, he said, 'You see this woman kneeling at my feet? When I came into your house as a guest you offered me no water for my feet. But she has watered them with her tears, and dried them with her hair.

'You gave me no kiss of peace. But she has not ceased kissing my feet.

'You did not anoint my head with oil. But she has anointed my feet with costly perfume.

'Her sins are many. But they are forgiven, for her love is great. One who has little to be forgiven will have little love.'

Then the Pharisees began to murmur among themselves. 'Who is this who even forgives sins? Only God can forgive sins.'

But Jesus said to Miriam, 'Your sins are forgiven. Go in peace.'

A Pharisee and a tax-collector

The parables of Jesus often turned things upside down. It was like that with a parable he told about God's forgiveness. It was a story of two men, one a Pharisee, the other a tax-collector. Both of them went to the Temple of Jerusalem to join in the afternoon service at 3 o'clock.

The Pharisee was a devout man, looked up to by the people. For he lived strictly by the sacred law of God, keeping it in every detail. That made him right with God, of course, and he was proud of his fine character and good deeds. He strode into the Temple and stood out in the open for his prayer, so that everyone could see him. He stretched out his arms, and raised both his hands and his eyes up to heaven, as the custom was for praying. It was the custom, too, to pray out loud, and not silently.

'God,' he said proudly, 'I thank you that I am not like other men. I do not cheat or steal. I am just and fair in all my dealings. I am faithful to my wife, and live purely. I'm certainly nothing like that tax-collector over there. I keep your law strictly, in every detail. Why, I even go beyond it. I go without food on both fast days, Monday and Thursday as well, every week. I give one tenth of everything I have to God — even a tenth of the herbs in my garden. No one could be more devout than I am!'

So the Pharisee went on, reminding God of all his good deeds. What a huge balance of goodness he had stored up with God!

The tax-collector had crept into a corner, where no one could see him. He knew that people hated and despised him. He knew that to them he was a traitor, collecting taxes for the Romans, and cheating at the same time. He knew that he was an outcast to both God and man.

He dared not even lift up his eyes to heaven. He stood with his head bowed, and beat his breast with his hand, in sorrow and despair at being so far from God.

He had no hope of being forgiven. He could only hope for God's mercy. Quietly, under his breath, he murmured the words of a psalm that he remembered: 'God, have mercy on me, sinner that I am, out of your great goodness. A humble and sorrowful heart, a broken spirit – these are the finest offerings. These you will not despise.'

Love and forgiveness

The ending of that parable shocked everyone who heard it. 'It was the tax-collector who was forgiven by God, not the Pharisee,' said Jesus. 'He went back to his home at peace with God. For God's mercy has no limits. His love has no bounds. Those who trust in themselves are far from him. Those who trust only in him are close to his heart.'

No wonder this parable shocked people. What wrong had the Pharisee done to be rejected by God? What good had the tax-collector done to be forgiven by God? Nothing at all. God judges men by their inner hearts, not by their outward actions. He can enter into a humble, broken heart. In a proud, hard heart there is no room for him.

Jesus the healer

WHAT WAS THE GOOD NEWS that Jesus brought? He proclaimed that the kingdom of God had come on earth. God ruled in the hearts of those who believed the Good News and gave themselves to him. Their hearts were changed, and they began a new life in his kingdom. How did Jesus show that God's kingdom had come? He showed it in himself.

He showed it in his teaching – in parables which taught that God is the loving Father of all.

He showed the power of God at work in his love for everyone, most of all for those who were despised as sinners.

He showed the power of God at work in his deeds of healing on those who were suffering in mind or body.

One of the temptations of Jesus had been to win men to God by doing great wonders and miracles. He would never do this. He healed people because of his love and sympathy for them. He did not want people to marvel when he healed them. Often he told them to keep it secret. His deeds of healing were signs of God's power at work among men. For God's kingdom had come.

A father who needed help

Capernaum was a fine center for the work of Jesus. From there he could travel out to the towns and villages of

56

Galilee. When he was in the town he stayed at the house of Simon Peter. The news soon spread when he arrived back, and a crowd quickly gathered at the door. They wanted to see Jesus, to hear his words, and to have his healing hands laid on their sick.

One day Jesus and some of his apostles came back to Capernaum by boat, for they had been to the other side of the lake. By the time they reached the shore a big crowd was waiting for Jesus. He sat in Peter's boat, just off the beach, to speak to them.

They were listening quietly when there was a sudden hubbub at the back of the crowd. Someone was trying to get through the crowd to reach Jesus. It was Jairus, a ruler of the synagogue. He was in charge of the services at the synagogue. He chose the men to read the lessons, to lead the prayers, and to address the congregation.

When Jairus reached the boat he fell on his knees, tears pouring down his face.

'Master,' he wept. 'It's my little daughter Rachel. She's very ill . . . I'm afraid she's dying. If only you will come and lay your hands on her I know she will live.'

'I will help you,' said Jesus tenderly.

'Rachel's only twelve years old . . . She's all I've got,' Jairus sobbed.

'I'll come at once,' said Jesus.

Jesus heals a woman

It was difficult to move toward the town, with the crowd all around Jesus. Among them was a woman who was determined to get close to him. She had been ill for many years, and no doctor had been able to cure her. When she heard of Jesus and his healing power she had made up her mind. 'If only I could just take hold of one of the tassels on his cloak I'm sure I'd be healed,' she said to herself.

At last she stood right behind Jesus. She bent down and gently took one of the tassels in her hand. At once she knew she was healed. But Jesus knew that power had gone out of him. He turned and said, 'Who touched my cloak?'

The disciples were astonished. 'Why do you ask who touched you, with the crowd jostling all around you?'

But the woman fell on her knees, trembling with fear, and told Jesus everything.

'Your faith has saved you,' said Jesus gently. 'Be healed, and go in peace.'

Jesus heals a little girl

Slowly Jesus and Jairus made their way to the narrow street where Jairus lived. Then a man came hurrying towards them. It was a servant of Jairus.

'Rachel is dead, sir,' he said. 'Why trouble the

Teacher any more? It's no use him coming now.'

'Don't be afraid,' Jesus said to Jairus. 'Just trust in me.'

Then Jesus turned to his disciples.

'Peter, James, John – come with me. The rest of you take the people down to the harbor, and I will return there.'

When they reached the house it was crowded with mourners. Many relatives and friends had come to share the grief of Jairus and his wife. They were lamenting noisily, some playing shrill, mournful music on flutes, others wailing aloud and rocking to and fro, as the custom was.

When Jesus came into the house the mourners stopped for a moment.

'Why are you making all this noise?' Jesus said to them. 'The child is not dead. She is sleeping.'

The mourners laughed at him. Was not Rachel lying pale and still, the life gone out of her?

Jesus spoke firmly to Jairus to get rid of the mourners. Then he went in to the little girl with her parents and the three apostles. He knelt by Rachel's bed, where she lay unconscious. Then Jesus took her hand and said, 'Little girl, it's time to wake up.'

Rachel sighed, and stirred, and opened her eyes. In a moment she was smiling and sitting up.

'Give her something to eat,' Jesus said to her parents. 'Make sure that you tell no one what has happened.'

Another father who needed help

On the hillside above Capernaum were the fine houses of rich and important people. There lived a nobleman named Chuza, his wife Joanna, and their little son named Philip. Chuza was the steward of King Herod who ruled over Galilee. Herod had built a new city named Tiberias, on the western shore of the Sea of Galilee, and made it his capital. So every morning Chuza had to leave home early to gallop the 9 miles to Tiberias for his work in the royal palace.

Chuza was busy all day long, looking after the palace and the servants, and the affairs of the king. Sometimes, when the king had a feast for important guests, he had to stay overnight at the palace. Most days he rode back in the early evening to his wife and son. As he drew near to Capernaum he looked up to his house on the hill, where Philip waited on the flat roof till he could see his father's horse. Then, as Chuza drew near, Philip would come running down the hill, and Chuza would swing him up on to his horse for the ride into the courtyard where Joanna waited.

One night Chuza was surprised to find that Philip

was not watching for him. Joanna waited for him in the courtyard with a troubled face. Philip was ill with a fever, hot and flushed and restless. Chuza knew the danger of fevers in a hot land. At once he ordered a servant to saddle a fresh horse and ride urgently to Tiberias for his good friend Alexander, the royal doctor.

It was dark by the time Alexander came. He was a skilful Greek doctor and he did all he could for Philip. All night they sat with him, bathing his forehead as he tossed and turned.

'We can only wait, and hope that the fever will break,' said the doctor. 'I'm sorry I can't do more.'

In the morning Alexander went back to Tiberias. 'He's the best doctor in the land,' Chuza said to his wife in despair. 'There's no one else.'

'There may be someone,' Joanna said. Then she told Chuza of all she had heard from the servants about Jesus the prophet and his healing power.

'I'll go to him,' said Chuza. 'Where is he?'

'He's staying in the town of Cana, the servants say.'

'I'll ride at once,' said Chuza, hurrying to saddle a horse.

Jesus heals a small boy

People stared at Chuza's fine horse, as he rode into the little town of Cana. They stared, too, at his royal uniform and rich cloak, when he made his way into the house where Jesus was speaking. What could a nobleman want with Jesus?

'Were you looking for me?' Jesus said in a kindly voice. Jesus was no ordinary man, Chuza could see that. He felt strangely tongue-tied.

'It's my son at Capernaum – a fever . . . he's dying. I beg you . . . heal him please!'

'People won't believe in me, unless I do signs and wonders,' said Jesus. 'I expect you are like that, too.'

Chuza was desperate. 'Please master! Come down with me now before my son dies!'

Then Jesus, seeing his faith, said to Chuza, 'Go in peace. Your son will live.'

And suddenly Chuza felt a great weight lift from him. He trusted Jesus with all his heart. He knew now that Philip would live.

A mother's way of thanking Jesus

Now Chuza had no time to lose. He must get swiftly to Tiberias for the royal banquet that evening, when Herod was entertaining Roman officers. But he felt calm and at peace as he rode over the hills. When he reached the palace he was far too busy to have any time to think. It was almost dawn before all the entertaining was over and his work done.

Chuza rode home as the sun came up over the hills. He was so tired, after two nights without sleep, but so peaceful too. As he came round the last bend in the road he saw servants hurrying to greet him.

'Master! Master!' they cried. 'Your son has recovered!'

'When did it happen?' Chuza asked eagerly.

'Yesterday, about one o'clock in the afternoon. Suddenly the fever left him – and there he was, full of life again!'

Then Chuza knew that it was at the very moment when Jesus had told him that his son would live. And, looking up toward the flat roof of his house, he saw Philip waving to him, Joanna by his side.

'Is there any way we can thank Jesus?' said Chuza to his wife when they were alone.

'Only by becoming his disciples,' said Joanna.

And Joanna was among those who helped Jesus as he made known the kingdom of God in his deeds and in his words.

Jesus the friend of children

ONE DAY JESUS AND HIS TWELVE APOSTLES were returning to the town of Capernaum, after a journey in the countryside. It happened that Jesus walked on ahead of them, busy with his thoughts. The apostles were busy talking to each other. Their talk was about the kingdom of God. When God's kingdom was set up on earth they were sure to be very important. Which of them would be the greatest? Who would be the most important of them all, they were wondering?

When they reached Capernaum they were glad to get to Peter's house to rest and to eat. But when they sat down Jesus said, 'What were you talking about, on the road?'

They were silent, for they felt ashamed. Jesus had often said that they were servants in the kingdom of God. They remembered one of his sayings, too: 'He who would be the greatest of all must be the servant of all.' But they had been imagining themselves as lords in the kingdom, not as servants.

Jesus knew their hearts, and he read the shame in their faces. It happened that small children were running in and out of the house, in their play. Jesus called to him a little curly-headed boy, sat him on his knee, and put his arms around him. Then he said to the twelve: 'No

61

one can enter into the kingdom of God unless he has the humble heart and the trusting faith of a child.'

That small boy was young David. He could not remember what had happened that day. But he never forgot the kind and loving face of the man who had sat him on his knee, the man called Jesus.

Boys at school

The day came when David saw that face again. It had started as quite an ordinary day. He had been woken up as usual by the sun-beams streaming through the cracks in the window-shutters, high in the wall. His sister Rachel was already washing, his mother getting breakfast, and his father loading up the donkey for his day's work. Soon they were sitting on mats for breakfast. They had milk to drink, butter and honey to eat with mother's crusty barley-bread, and figs, dates and raisins for fruit.

Then David hurried out, called next door for his friend Peter, and they set off for school. It was held in the courtyard of the synagogue where the boys sat in a circle around their teacher in the warm sunshine. They practised writing their letters in the sand with sticks. When they knew them well they would begin to read the precious scrolls of the Sacred Writings kept in the synagogue.

David and Peter walked into the courtyard and bowed to their teacher.

'God be with you,' he said in greeting.

'And with you, sir,' said the boys before sitting down with their friends.

Girls at home and at play

Rachel stayed at home with her mother, for only boys went to school. She was learning from mother how to clean, and cook, and sew, and how to look after her baby sister.

Their house was one big room, with a platform at one end where the family lived and slept. The animals spent the night on the floor below, with the family donkey tied to his manger by the wall. Rachel and her mother began their work with tidying up the platform. They rolled up the mattresses on which the family slept, and put them away in the alcove in the wall. Then they wrapped up the baby snugly in swaddling bands, wrapped round and round, and laid her on clean straw in the manger. There she would be warm and cosy and safe. Then there was the floor to be swept, and water to be fetched from the well to fill the big earthenware water-jar. Now Mother was ready to bake the day's bread, and Rachel helped her to grind the barley grain for flour. Now she was free to play with her friend Rebecca next door.

'Let's play pebbles,' said Rachel, when they met outside. They drew squares in the sand and wrote numbers in each square. They threw a pebble into each square in turn, and then hopped after it. But their hopscotch soon made them hot, and they decided to go up on the roof to play.

Each house had a stairway outside which led up to the flat roof. A roof was made of beams, laid across the tops of the walls, and filled in with brushwood and clay to make it firm and level. The parapet around the roof made sure that no one could fall off. Here the girls could sit and play, and the houses were so close that they could easily go from one roof to the other.

First they played a game, putting small pebbles on their palms, throwing them up into the air, and seeing how many they could catch on the back of their hands. When they grew tired of games they decided to sit quiet, and model some more clay animals for the farm which they were making in a corner of the roof.

Boys at play

The boys dashed out of the courtyard when school was over at noon. 'Come on!' Peter called to David. 'Let's go down by the river.' They dashed down to the stream, tugging their slings out of the wide girdles round their waists, which made fine pockets.

'That tree over there,' said David. 'Three hits wins.'

They had each made their slings from a piece of goatskin, with a leather string at each end. Each of them in turn took a small round pebble from the stream, and put it in the hollowed center of the skin. Then, holding the strings, he twirled the sling round and round his head, and then suddenly let one string go so that the pebble flew to its target.

'I'm going to make a new pipe,' said Peter, when they had had enough of slinging. 'My old one has split.'

'All right,' said David. 'I'll make a double pipe.'

They made their pipes from reeds growing by the water, using the small knives kept handy in their girdles. Each of them chose a reed and bored holes in it, and, when it was finished, made notes by putting a finger over each hole in turn. David made his double pipe from two reeds, each cut and bored separately, and then bound together.

Now it was time for dinner, and the boys made their way home, playing tunes on their new pipes.

Girls and boys playing together

After dinner the four children went to the market-place. There was always something exciting to see there. It was the open ground, just inside the town wall. Everything happened there – farmers selling their fruits and vegetables; traders shouting out the goods they had for sale; law cases being tried; travelling merchants with their camels, bringing news from afar; town meetings; business deals, made with lots of haggling; children playing games; townsfolk chatting and gossiping and telling friends their news.

The children soon met some of their friends. They **decided to play weddings. First a bride and bridegroom** had to be chosen, and dressed up ready for the great occasion. Then the boys formed the wedding procession. For it was the men who did the special dancing and singing at a wedding – a round dance, with stamping of feet and clapping of hands. The girls sat on the sand, making their music and setting the rhythm, with hand-drums, rattles, cymbals and clappers, while some of the boys made jolly tunes with their flutes and pipes.

After playing at weddings they naturally played at funerals. Now it was the turn of the girls, for it was the women who did the mourning at funerals. They wailed aloud, rocking to and fro, with groans and shrieks and loud laments, while the boys played shrill, mournful music on their pipes and flutes.

Squabbles at play

But it was not all fun. The children often squabbled among themselves, with tiffs and sulks and tears. Jesus loved children, he knew their games – and he knew how they squabbled. He spoke about it to the people.

'You people are like children, playing at weddings and funerals,' he said. 'You complain just like they do. "It's not fair," they say to each other. "When we play a wedding jig you won't dance. When we pipe a lament you won't wail and beat your breasts."

'You people are just like that. John the Baptist came out of the desert, stern and fierce. "He's a raving madman," you said. Then I came, sharing the life of ordinary people in their homes. "He's no prophet," you said. "He's too fond of eating and drinking and mixing with sinners."

'You're never satisfied, are you. John came to herald the kingdom of God. I came to bring the kingdom of God. And all you can do is to find fault and complain, just like children in their play.'

Jesus welcomes children

While the children were playing, that afternoon, a group of travellers came into the market-place. The children glanced at them out of curiosity, and David saw again the face that he remembered so well. At once he dashed off home, for his mother had often said how much she longed to see Jesus the prophet. He found her with Peter's mother, working together at their embroidery.

64

'Jesus the prophet!' he gasped out. 'He's in the market-place!'

At once the two mothers dropped their work and hastened back with David. By now a big crowd had gathered around Jesus. They joined the crowd with their children, and tried to pass through to get near to Jesus. But his fussy apostles stopped them.

'Don't bother Jesus now,' they said. 'You can see how busy he is. Besides, he's walked a long way and he's very tired.'

The mothers were sad and disappointed to be turned away. Then, suddenly, the voice of Jesus rang out angrily.

'Let the children come to me!' he ordered. 'Do not forbid them!'

The two mothers turned back, and saw Jesus looking sternly at his apostles. The people made way for them, and they came to Jesus, bringing Rachel and Rebecca, David and Peter. And Jesus took each child in his arms, one after the other, and blessed them. They could not understand who he was. But they knew that he was the friend of children.

Our Father who art in heaven

LEVI LIVED A QUIET LIFE in his village, tucked away in the hills of Galilee. He and his wife Mary had not been blessed with children, and they seldom had a visitor. So it was quite exciting when one night there was a loud knock on his door, just as Levi was getting ready for bed. 'Benjamin! My dear old friend!' cried Levi when he opened the door. They embraced each other warmly, and shared the kiss of greeting, before Levi welcomed his visitor into the house.

'I'm on my way to Capernaum,' Benjamin explained. 'I planned to reach the town tonight and put up at the inn. But I was slower than I thought, and it was getting so late. I thought of you, and of the joy of seeing you – quite apart from getting a bed for the night.'

Of course Levi was delighted to welcome his old friend. But he would have welcomed a stranger, too. For the law of hospitality was sacred – no one would refuse food and drink and shelter to a traveller in need. For if he were turned away, in a hot and thirsty land, his life might well be in danger.

So Levi had every reason to welcome Benjamin into his home. They had lots to talk about, and all their news to share. As soon as they had sat down Levi called his wife to get bread and wine for the honored guest. How horrified Levi was when Mary had to say that there was not a crumb of bread left in the house. Like every housewife, she baked bread every day – for it quickly went bad in the heat. She baked just enough for the two of them – and, of course, she had no idea that a guest was coming. Nor were there any bread-shops in a small village like theirs.

Levi was aghast. What on earth could he do? It would be an awful disgrace to break the law of hospitality. And how ashamed he would be when everyone heard about it. He must do something. There was only one thing for it. He must borrow some bread from Simeon, his best friend, who lived on the other side of the village. He hurried off to Simeon's house as fast as his legs could carry him.

How a friend got bread

Simeon had been blessed with a large family. He was a good father to his children, and strict too. He made sure that they got to bed in good time at night. First he brought the donkey in, and tied it to the manger. Then he shut his door, and bolted it tight with the heavy bar of wood which only he could lift, fixing it in the sockets on the two doorposts. Then he made sure that the clay lamp had been filled with olive oil, and the flaxen wick trimmed, so that the lamp would keep alight all night. For no one liked being in the dark, and there was always the danger of thieves.

By now his wife and children had got out the beds and spread them over the platform where the family slept. They were mattresses, filled with straw, and with Simeon's big family the whole platform was covered with them. So he had to clamber over the children's mattresses to reach his own, and settle down for the night. Sleep was a gift from God – so to lie awake was really a sin. Simeon made sure that no one lay awake in his family, least of all himself. Soon all was quiet and still in his house, and Simeon drifted off to sleep.

Then it happened. It was about midnight. Suddenly there came a loud crash on Simeon's door. Someone was thumping it like a madman. Who on earth could it be, at that time of night? Simeon, only half awake, tried to ignore it. Perhaps the madman would go away. But he didn't. The banging got worse. Then Simeon heard a voice: 'Simeon! Simeon! It's your friend Levi! A visitor has come – I've no bread for his supper! Lend me three loaves! Please! Please!'

Simeon sat up, very cross at being so rudely disturbed.

'Go away!' he cried. 'The door is barred. My family are in bed. I can't disturb them now. Leave us in peace!'

But Levi was desperate. He must get bread. Just three

small loaves would be enough for his visitor. Simeon's wife always baked spare bread, with her big family – and Simeon hadn't denied that they had some.

'Three loaves!' Levi yelled, banging away. 'Just three loaves!'

Levi was quite without any shame. He just went on, banging and yelling. By now the whole family were awake. There'd be no peace till Levi got what he wanted.

Simeon could stand no more. He got up angrily, clambered over his children, grabbed three loaves, got the door open, and thrust them at his friend. He gave Levi no time to say thank you before slamming the door. As for Levi, he hurried home happily with his precious loaves. Simeon had not given him the loaves because they were friends. Levi had only got them by being persistent – by going on asking and asking till he got what he wanted.

Talking to God

Jesus often left his disciples and went off to be alone. But they knew that he was not alone, at those times. He was with the heavenly Father, talking to him in prayer. They longed to feel close to God too. One day, when Jesus came back from praying, they said to him, 'Lord, teach us to pray, just as John the Baptist taught his disciples to pray.'

Jesus told them this parable. Like every parable, it only taught one thing. It did not mean that God is like grumpy Simeon, who did not want to be disturbed. Its lesson was that Levi got what he wanted by going on asking and asking.

'Be like that,' said Jesus to his disciples. 'Go on asking the heavenly Father for your needs. Look how you fathers give good things to your children. How much more will the heavenly Father give his good things to those who go on asking.'

Jesus did not mean that prayer is just asking God for things. There are many other things to say to him – things like saying thank you, and saying sorry, and, of course, asking him to give his good things to others who are in need. Jesus showed that by giving his disciples a pattern prayer. Followers of Jesus call it the Lord's Prayer:

> Our Father who art in heaven,
> Hallowed be thy name.
> Thy kingdom come,
> Thy will be done
> On earth as it is in heaven.
> Give us this day our daily bread,
> And forgive us our debts,
> As we also forgive our debtors;
> And lead us not into temptation,
> But deliver us from evil.

So prayer is not asking God to do what we want. It is asking that God's will may be done, so that his kingdom may come.

How a widow got justice

Every Jewish town had a law-court. Jewish laws were sacred, for they came from God. Rules for the law-court made sure that everyone was treated fairly, and that justice was done. But everything depended on the judges. They were older, wiser, devout men, chosen carefully. They were not paid. For seeing that justice was done was a fine way of serving both God and man, without any thought of reward.

But money could come into it. Officers of the court might accept money from a wealthy man, even if the judge was strictly honest. He could pay the court officer to get his case heard quickly. A poor man would have to wait, for he could not afford to pay a bribe. It would be far worse if the judge was dishonest and took bribes. For then he would see that the rich man won his case. There would be no justice for the poor in his court.

It was like that in a certain town. The judge was an evil man who did not care about giving justice. A poor widow came to his court. She was being cheated by a rich and powerful man. She had no husband or son to help her. There were laws to protect widows – but any rascal could get round them. That is why the Jews had a saying that caring for widows and orphans was a test of true religion. The widow was helpless without a man to stand up for her – and without money to bribe the court officer, let alone the rascally judge. The rich man cheating her would win in the end simply by bribing the judge.

The widow decided that her only hope of getting justice was to be persistent – to keep on asking the evil judge to hear her case. She gave him no peace. Every morning she was back again at his court, and every evening outside his house.

'Give me justice!' she kept crying out. 'This man is cheating me!' She was determined to wear the judge down till she got what she wanted.

In the end the judge could stand no more. 'I'm not afraid of God or of men, let alone widows,' he said to himself. 'But this is too much. I never get a moment's peace, day or night, from this wretched widow. I can't stand any more of it. There's only one way to stop her pestering me – I'll give her what she wants.'

Jesus himself showed what this parable meant. The poor widow got justice by pestering the hard-hearted judge. How much more then will God be ready to hear the poor and needy when they cry to him! For he is the tender and loving Father, eager to hear his children and to answer their prayers, when they cry to him for justice and peace on earth.

70

Forgive us...
as we forgive

SIMON PETER was a big, bluff, burly man. He spoke like that, too. He had strong feelings and he showed them easily. He spoke without thinking, and he was quick-tempered. He often got angry with Andrew, his brother, who was quiet and slow. When he cooled off he was sorry. He knew that he ought to forgive Andrew, but he found it very hard. One day Peter stormed up to Jesus in a temper. 'How often do I have to forgive this brother of mine?' he demanded. 'Until seven times?'

Peter knew what the Rabbis taught about forgiveness. Men should be forgiving, just as God is. But they are human, so to forgive three times was as much as could be expected. Somehow Peter knew that this would not be enough for Jesus. That was why he said 'seven times', not 'three times'. Surely that would be enough?

But Jesus answered, 'Not seven times, Peter. Seventy times seven.'

This was a Jewish way of speaking. It did not mean 490 times. It meant that Peter should go on forgiving, just as God goes on forgiving – without any limit at all.

Jesus told a parable to explain what he meant.

The governor who cheated

There was once a great emperor who ruled over many lands. His huge empire spread far and wide. He could not

71

possibly rule it by himself. He appointed a governor to rule over each land. He chose able men who would rule wisely and firmly. For each governor had to make sure that the emperor's laws were obeyed, and that there was peace and order in his land. He had to collect the taxes for the emperor, too. So each governor had to be honest and trustworthy. Most important of all, he must be loyal to the emperor, and serve him faithfully.

The governor was the most powerful man in the land which he ruled. For he represented the emperor himself. He could easily become proud, and forget that he owed his position to the emperor, and was always responsible to him. For the emperor left his governors to rule over their lands without bothering them. He trusted them.

It was like that for several years. Then, suddenly, the emperor decided to see if the governors were being faithful to him. He summoned all of them to the royal palace, in his capital city. He had decided to have their accounts examined, to make sure that they had been sending all the taxes due to the royal exchequer.

That was how a certain governor was found out. He had been cheating the emperor, year after year, by keeping back some of the tax money for himself. His debt to the emperor had mounted up, and now it had reached the enormous sum of 10,000 gold talents. A talent was a certain weight of gold, and it was the most valuable sum of money known in those days. The number 10,000 was the biggest number known, too. So it was a huge, impossible debt that the governor owed to the emperor because of his cheating. It might be around $125 million in our money today.

The governor is forgiven

The emperor was furious when he found out how the governor had been deceiving him, cheating him, and betraying his trust.

'Sell him as a slave!' he ordered. 'Sell his wife and his children too. Sell his houses and his lands. Sell everything he owns to pay his debt!'

Even selling everything would not pay off much of that huge debt. But all the emperor could think of was punishing the wretch as hard as possible. Anyway, it was only fair that he should pay back all he could toward his wicked debt.

The proud governor was terrified. It was the end of everything for him. He threw himself on the ground before the whole royal court, and all the other governors. He grovelled at the emperor's feet, weeping and groaning, pleading for mercy.

'Have patience, Lord,' he wept. 'I'll pay back every penny I owe.'

72

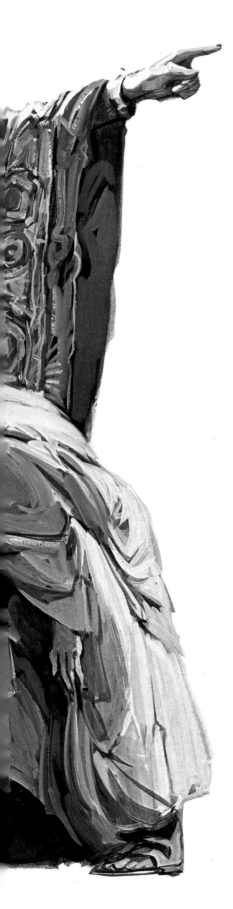

He could never really pay back his huge debt. The emperor knew that well enough. But he felt sorry for the rich, proud governor grovelling at his feet. He did not even condemn him for being so foolish, so greedy, so dishonest, so disloyal. He simply forgave the governor his whole, huge, impossible debt.

The governor does not forgive

The governor was still trembling as he went down the palace steps, out into the market place. What a relief! What a terrible fate he had faced!

Then, by chance, he noticed someone he knew in the crowd. Yes, it was one of his own officials. And the rascal owed him 100 silver coins, didn't he?

'Pay your debts!' he shouted, seizing the poor man by the collar.

The poor man threw himself on the ground, grovelling at the governor's feet.

'Have patience, Lord,' he wept. 'I'll pay back every penny I owe.'

His debt was about $50. Although he was a poor man he could pay it back, bit by bit. It was not an impossible debt – like, say, $125 million.

But the governor had no pity. He showed no mercy. He had the man thrown into the debtors' prison.

Forgiving and being forgiven

The story of what had happened soon spread. Servants at the royal palace heard about it. They were horrified, for they knew how the governor had been forgiven by the emperor. It was not long before the emperor himself heard about it. At once he sent for the governor.

'You wicked servant!' he said. 'I forgave you all your huge debt to me – but you could not forgive your servant the tiny debt he owed to you.

'Very well! I will treat you exactly as you treated your servant. You will go to the debtors' prison where you sent him. You will stay there, under the jailers, until you have repaid every penny of your debt to me.'

The governor could never repay his huge debt. He would suffer in prison for the rest of his life.

Our debt to God

It is like that between you and God, Jesus was saying in this parable. You owe him a huge, impossible debt which you can never repay. He loves to forgive, in his loving kindness. But he cannot show mercy to you unless you show mercy to others. You must forgive, if you want to be forgiven.

When you pray to God say:

'Forgive us our debts,
As we also forgive our debtors.'

Love your neighbor

JEWS LIVE BY THE SACRED LAWS which came to them from God, through their prophets. In the time of Jesus there were men called Scribes who were experts in these laws. One of the questions they often talked about was – which is the most important law of all? Some said it was the commandment to keep the sabbath day holy and set apart to God. Some said it was the commandment against making idols and worshipping them. Devout men called Pharisees, who kept every detail of the sacred laws, said it was the commandment to give one-tenth of all your possessions to God.

One day there was a Scribe among the people listening to Jesus. He decided to find out what Jesus thought about this question.

'Teacher,' he said, 'which commandment is the greatest of all?'

Jesus said to him, 'Love is the greatest commandment of all. Love God, with all your heart and soul and mind and strength. Love your neighbor as yourself. There is no commandment greater than these. If you live by them you will be keeping all the sacred laws, and all the teachings of the prophets.'

Now the Scribe loved to argue, and he wanted to show how clever he was. He asked another question:

'But who is my neighbor?'

This was a fine question. 'Neighbor' means 'nigh-dweller', someone who lives near to you. But the law to 'love your neighbor' could not mean only the people in your own street, or village, or town. Jewish teachers said that it meant everyone who was a Jew. So Jews should show love to all people of their own race. But what about people of other races? What about people of other religions? What about enemies? What did Jesus think about these questions?

Jesus did not argue with the clever Scribe. He told a parable.

The man who fell among thieves

One day a certain Jew went down from Jerusalem to Jericho. The road ran for 18 miles through wild and lonely hills from Jerusalem, high on its hill, to Jericho in its low-lying valley. So it was downhill all the way. But it was more of a rough track than a road. Jews did not bother about making good roads, as the Romans did.

The Jew was asking for trouble, travelling alone on the winding track through the desolate hills. Huge boulders and hidden caves made fine hiding-places for robbers. It was always a dangerous road. In the time of Jesus it was called 'the red road', for so much blood was shed there. Gangs of wild brigands lived in the hills, waiting to waylay travellers and rob them of everything they had.

That was exactly what happened to the unfortunate Jew. Robbers leaped out on him, and it was soon over. They even tore off his clothes. They left him on the road, savagely wounded, and half-dead.

Priest and Levite pass by

The only hope for the helpless Jew was that someone might come along the lonely road and take pity on him. By chance someone did come, hurrying toward Jerusalem. He was a priest of the Temple in the holy city, a man whose whole life was dedicated to the service of God. When he saw his fellow Jew lying there, half-dead, he hurried even more quickly. He kept his distance, and passed by on the other side of the track.

Some time later there came another traveller. He too was a Jew and a holy man. For he was a Levite, one of the servants of the Temple who assisted the priests in the worship of God. He too saw his fellow Jew lying there, half-dead. He too kept his distance, and passed by on the other side of the track.

Both the priest and the Levite could have had good reasons for not trying to save their fellow Jew. One good excuse was that the robbers might still be near. They would only put themselves in danger by lingering there.

But there was another important reason. The wounded Jew might be already dead – and anyone who touched a dead body was defiled and impure. He would have to go through long religious ceremonies to be made pure again, and fit to take part in the worship of God. Both the priest and the Levite would be banned from the Temple if they tried to help and found the man already dead.

There was another reason, too. Many Jews believed that suffering was sent by God as a punishment for sin. It was his judgement upon a man who had offended against him. So the wounded Jew's suffering might have been sent by God.

Jesus did not say anything against the priest and the Levite. They were simply useless. They were good men according to their religion. It was their religion that was **wrong. It had nothing to do with loving a neighbor.** They left their fellow Jew to a lingering death.

The good Samaritan

But a third man happened to come along the road. He was not a Jew, so he had no duty to help the wounded Jew. In fact he was a Samaritan, and his people had been bitter enemies of the Jews for 400 years. The Samaritans were partly Jews by race, and they had their own Temple for the worship of God. But Jews regarded all Samaritans as foreigners, and pagans, and enemies.

The land where the Samaritans lived lay between Galilee in the north and Jerusalem in the south. Jews travelling from north to south would never go near the territory of the Samaritans. Instead, they took the long route round by the river Jordan in order to avoid them.

Things had got even worse in the time of Jesus. One night, when he was a boy, a group of Samaritans had crept into the sacred Temple at Jerusalem. They threw the bones of dead men around the court of the Temple so as to defile it.

The crowd of Jews, listening to Jesus, must have bristled when Jesus brought a Samaritan into his story. But worse was to come – the Samaritan was the hero of his parable.

The Samaritan was full of sympathy when he saw the Jew lying by the track, half-dead. At once he got off his donkey to help. He used his flask of oil to bathe the Jew's wounds. He opened his wine-bottle and used his wine to stop the bleeding, and to quench the poor man's thirst. He tore strips off his tunic to make bandages and bind up the wounds. He risked his own life, too, lingering there on the lonely road. But he did not hurry. Carefully he lifted the wounded Jew on to his donkey, and supported him there, as they went slowly along the

road toward the inn which he knew lay ahead.

There was only one inn on the road from Jerusalem to Jericho. It was not like a hotel. An inn was simply a square courtyard, with a wall around it, and a covered building. Well-to-do travellers could hire one of the rooms in the building. Others just laid out their mattresses under the wooden roof, after tethering their animals in the courtyard. Travellers brought their own bedding and food and drink. The innkeeper had to be paid for any service he provided.

The Samaritan hired a room for the wounded Jew. When he left the next morning he took out his purse.

'Here are two silver coins,' he said to the innkeeper. 'Take care of my friend for me, and see that he has whatever he needs until he is well again. If you spend more than that I will repay you on my return journey.'

Love as God loves

When Jesus finished his parable he turned to the Scribe. 'Which of these three men was neighbor to the wounded Jew, do you think?'

The Scribe hated even to say the word Samaritan. 'The man who was kind to him,' he replied.

'Then you have answered your own question,' said Jesus. 'Go your way, and be a good neighbor yourself.'

Jesus was teaching something quite new. The priest and the Levite believed that it was more important to serve God by offering sacrifices in the Temple than by offering love to the needy. Jesus was teaching that God wanted loving kindness from his worshippers. Jews believed that foreigners were outside God's love. Jesus was teaching that God's love has no limits – nor should the love of his worshippers. Your neighbor, Jesus was teaching, is everyone.

Jesus gave his disciples a new law: 'The old law said that you should love your neighbor and hate your enemy. I give you a new law. Love your enemies, bless those who curse you, pray for those who are cruel to you. Then you will be sons of your heavenly Father. For he does not pick and choose whom he will love. His love goes out to all his children. He makes his sun rise on the evil and on the good. He sends rain on the just and on the unjust. What is specially good about loving those who love you? Don't the people you despise as sinners do that? You must love everyone, just as God loves everyone, if you want to be his children.'

Faithful stewards

I N THE LAND OF GALILEE, where Jesus lived and taught, there were rich people as well as poor peasants. A wealthy man needed servants to look after his household and his lands. His servants belonged to him and to his estate. But they were nothing like the slaves of the Romans. Roman slaves had no laws to protect them, so that their masters could treat them as they liked. They were the property of their masters. They might be treated well. They might be treated cruelly, or killed. It was quite different among the Jews. Jewish servants had laws to protect them, and in any case they could be given their freedom. A Jewish servant was one of the family, and his master's house was home. It was far better to be a servant in a good home than to be a free man starving in the streets.

Servants could become quite important, and be given a lot of responsibility by their masters. It was like that, said Jesus, with a certain rich man who was going on a journey. What should he do with all his money, while he was away from home? A poorer man buried it in the ground, so that only he would know where it was hidden. A rich man could store it away in his house – but that would be an invitation to thieves.

The best thing to do was to deposit the money with

bankers in the town. They were really money-changers, for different kinds of money were used in the land of Israel. There was money of the Greeks and Romans and Phoenicians, as well as Jewish money, and coins of rulers like King Herod. The bankers lent out the different kinds of money, and charged good interest for their loans. Then they paid back some of the interest they had gained to the rich men who deposited money with them.

This rich man had a huge sum of money, so he would have got a lot of interest from bankers. But there was another way, by which his money could earn a lot more than interest from bankers. He decided to leave it with servants. He would trust them to trade with it, and to make as much money as they could for him while he was away.

Servants put on trust
When the time came for him to depart on his journey the rich master called in his three best servants.

'I have to go away on a journey,' he said to them. 'I am going to trust you with my money while I am away. Use it well, and make as much money as you can for me.'

On the table in front of him there were eight bags of gold, each of the same weight. This weight of gold or silver was called a talent, and it was worth a certain amount of money. A talent of silver was worth about $2,500 in our money, and a talent of gold was worth about $25,000. So each bag was worth a great deal.

The master knew what each of his servants was capable of doing, so he gave them different amounts. Jacob, his best servant, was given five bags. Benjamin, his next best servant, was given two talents. Reuben, not as capable as the others, was given one talent. Then their master went off on his journey, leaving them to do their best for him. It would be a good test of their loyalty to him.

Jacob was proud to be trusted by his master, and was eager to please him. He soon showed his ability for big business. He joined in with the merchants who traded in costly luxuries from abroad – scents and spices from Arabia, silks from the East, fine damask cloth from Damascus. He was hardworking, as well as clever. By the time his master was due to return he had doubled the money entrusted to him.

Benjamin traded busily, too. He knew he was not clever enough to compete with the merchants selling luxuries from abroad. He traded in the home market, buying and selling corn and oil, salt fish and dried fruits. He, too, doubled the money entrusted to him.

Reuben buried his bag of money in the ground. Only

he knew where it was, so he was keeping it quite safe for his master.

Servants get their reward

At last the great day came, and the master returned home. There was hurry and bustle all through the house, and a fine supper was prepared for him. When he was sat down at table he sent for the three servants to give account for the talents he had entrusted to them.

Jacob came in eagerly and put his ten bags on the table. 'Look, master!' he said proudly. 'I have doubled your money! Here are ten talents for you!'

'Well done, Jacob!' said his master. 'You are a good and faithful servant. You have always worked well for me. Now you have proved yourself worthy of much more responsibility. I am giving you your freedom, and making you my chief steward. Come, share my feast, sit down with me as a free man and a friend.'

Then Benjamin came forward eagerly and put his four bags on the table. 'Master, you entrusted me with two talents. Look! I have doubled your money! Here are four talents for you!'

'Well done, Benjamin!' said his master. 'You too have proved yourself a good and faithful servant, and worthy of more responsibility. I am giving you your freedom, and making you my second steward. Come, share my feast, sit down with me as a free man and a friend.'

Then Reuben came forward, and dumped his one talent safely on the table. 'I knew what a hard man you are, master,' he said, ready with his excuses. 'You reap sheaves which you have not sown, and gather in corn which you have not sifted. I knew how angry you'd be if I used your money and lost it. So I hid it in the earth, to keep it safe. Here it is, just as you gave it to me.'

His master was very angry. 'You lazy rascal!' he cried. 'So you knew I was a hard man, did you? Then you should have lodged my money with the bankers. At least I'd have got interest from them. From you I get nothing! Here, take the talent from him,' he ordered. 'Give it to my friend here who was entrusted with five talents, and doubled them by his hard work. And throw that useless wretch out into the night!'

Talents and gifts

In this parable Jesus was likening the master to God, and the servants to different kinds of men. God had entrusted his people with knowledge of himself, through their prophets. Some used it busily, and spread abroad their knowledge of God. Others kept it safe and hid it, so that God received nothing from them.

We still use the word talent. It means any special ability which a person has. For example, it might be talent for music, or art, or sport, or study, or games, or friendship, or caring for others. We call it a 'gift', too, saying that a person has a gift for one of these things.

Both these words, 'talent' and 'gift', mean that something has been entrusted to us, just as the talents were entrusted to the three servants. We are to use our talents, not to hide and bury them. The more we use them the more they grow. They have been entrusted to us by God and we must use them in his service and in the service of others.

Good and bad stewards

A Jewish servant was one of the household, and his master's house was home. Far better to be a servant there than a free man homeless and hungry. But best of all was to be the master's steward, like Jacob in the parable.

The steward of the household was a very important person. Everyone knew him by the big keys of his master's house which hung proudly from his girdle. He had the complete trust of his master. He acted for his master, and represented him, so that he had great power. He was even more important when his master was away from home. For then he was in charge of the whole household. Nothing would show more clearly what kind of steward he was.

'What is a good steward like?' said Jesus, in another parable. 'He is always faithful and loyal to his master. He is wise and tireless in doing his duties. When his master is away from home he behaves exactly as if his master was there. When his master returns he sees how well the steward has cared for the servants and run the household. He is full of praise, and rewards him with even more responsibility. "I am putting you in charge of my whole estate," he says. Now the steward is in charge of his master's fields, too.

'But what is a bad steward like?' Jesus went on. 'When his master is away he says to himself, "This is my big chance! The master won't be back for ages! I can do just as I like." His power goes to his head. He lolls at his master's table, eating his best food, drinking his best wine – drunk most of the day. He lords it over the other servants, beating them, and treating them cruelly.

'Then, suddenly, when the puffed-up steward least expects it, his master returns. The steward had no idea that he would be returning that day, let alone at that hour. His master catches him out – drunk at his table, ill-treating the servants he is supposed to be caring for, lording it over them.

'The master deals with him exactly as he deserves. He gives him a good beating, and throws him out of his house.

'For much is expected from those to whom much is given.'

Stewards of God

Jesus often likened his disciples to stewards of God. They have been entrusted with life and with talents. They are to be used in loving God and loving our **neighbor. A good and faithful steward will always be** busy in the service of his master, and in doing his master's will.

82

Be prepared

JESUS WAS A FRIEND TO EVERYONE – rich people and poor people, devout men and despised outcasts. He shared in every part of their lives, both the good times and the bad. The happiest times of all were weddings. Jesus went to weddings – and he told parables about them too. A wedding was arranged by the fathers of the young couple. They met together at the house of the bride and made the agreement. The young man and the young woman were betrothed to each other solemnly. The bridegroom paid an agreed sum to his bride and to her father. His present to the bride was often made into a circlet of coins which she wore round her forehead, over her head-dress.

The betrothal of the young couple lasted for a year. To be betrothed was just as binding as being married. Then, at the end of the year, came the happy wedding festivities. They lasted for a week, and they usually took place in the autumn. For by then the harvest had been safely gathered in, and everyone was free to join in the week of wedding celebrations.

The wedding feast was held in the evening, and it took place at the house of the bridegroom. There the feast was prepared. There the bridegroom's friends, called his groomsmen, came together to help him get ready.

It was like that too in the house of the bride.
Her friends, called bridesmaids, gathered there to help her
dress for the wedding feast. When they were all ready
they waited for the coming of the bridegroom and his
groomsmen to fetch the bride. Then came the happy
procession of bride and bridegroom, bridesmaids and
groomsmen, to the bridegroom's house for the wedding
feast. As it was evening the procession was lit up, and
this was the duty of the bridesmaids. Each of them
carried a small clay lamp, with a wick burning in olive
oil, just like the lamps used in the home.

Now the bridesmaids did not know when the
bridegroom and his groomsmen would arrive. It might be
a long wait, even two or three hours. Bridesmaids had to
keep their lamps alight all the time, for it was not easy
to light them quickly when the bridegroom arrived. But
this meant that they were using up the oil in their
lamps. So sensible bridesmaids always brought a flask of
extra oil with them. For it would be very shameful if
their lamps flickered and went out just when they were
needed for the procession. While they waited they
chatted or dozed. When the shouting told them that the
bridegroom was coming they had only to refill their
lamps, and trim the wicks, and they were ready for the
procession.

Wise and foolish bridesmaids

Now it happened at a certain wedding, said Jesus, that
the bridegroom and groomsmen were very late. The bride
had ten bridesmaids waiting with her. Five of them were
sensible girls. But the other five were foolish and
thoughtless – they had not brought extra oil with them.
All of them had fallen asleep, during their long wait.
Then suddenly, about midnight, they were woken up
with a start. 'The bridegroom's coming!' was the happy
cry. The five sensible girls soon had their lamps filled
and trimmed. But the lamps of the foolish girls were
already flickering low, for their oil was almost gone.

'Give us some of your oil – our lamps are going out!'
they cried to the sensible bridesmaids.

'We dare not,' they replied. 'For then we might not
have enough for our own lamps during the procession.
You'll have to go and fetch some more oil for your
lamps.'

The five thoughtless girls hurried off. While they were
gone the happy procession went on its way to the house
of the bridegroom. Now all the guests were there and the
wedding-feast could begin. So the watchman was ordered
to shut the door, and to put the heavy bar across it, so
as to keep out any unwelcome visitors. Soon the joyful

feasting was in full swing.

Then came loud banging at the door, and noisy cries from outside. It was the five foolish bridesmaids.

'Lord! Lord! Open to us!' they cried. 'We are bridesmaids! Let us in!'

But the bridegroom called out, 'All my guests are here with me. The feast has started, and the door is barred. I don't want any strangers at my wedding feast.'

Guests at a feast

In that parable of Jesus the wedding feast was likened to the kingdom of God. Jesus invited people to enter into God's kingdom. Some of them were sensible and prepared themselves for it. Others were thoughtless and careless about it. They risked being shut out from the kingdom of God.

Another parable told of guests who were thoughtless and careless. They had been invited to a banquet given by a rich man. He prepared a fine feast for them. When everything was ready he sent his servant round to the guests to tell them it was time to come. But they all made excuses.

'I have just bought a field,' said one guest to the servant. 'I must go out and inspect it. Please excuse me.'

'I have bought five yoke of oxen,' said another. 'I simply must go and examine them. Please excuse me.'

'I have just been married,' said another. 'I cannot leave my young bride all alone. Please excuse me.'

So it went on.

The servant came back and reported all the excuses to his master. He was very angry.

'Go out quickly into the town,' he ordered his servant. 'You'll find beggars in the streets and lanes – poor, maimed, blind, lame. Bring them in to my feast.'

The servant hurried out and brought in all the beggars he could find.

'There are still some empty seats,' he told his master.

'Then go out further – into the lanes and byways of the countryside. Make them come. I'm determined to have my house filled. None of the men I invited will enjoy my banquet. Others will enjoy it instead.'

God's kingdom was like that banquet, too. God had sent prophets to his chosen people to proclaim the coming of his kingdom. He had sent his servant, John the Baptist, to announce that everything was ready and the time had come. Now Jesus had brought God's kingdom. But many were making excuses. So others would take their place – people despised as sinners, outcasts like tax-collectors, and those who did not live strictly by the sacred law.

Counting the cost of building

Jesus often spoke of God's invitation to men to enter his kingdom. But they must count the cost.

'Suppose that a man is going to build a big tower,' said Jesus. 'First he sits down, makes his plans, and works out the cost of his building. What would happen if he did not work out his costs? He gets halfway through his building and finds he has run out of money. Then he has to abandon it. How people will mock at him, and laugh at his folly. "He started to build, but he couldn't finish it!" they'll say.'

Everyone knew whom Jesus was talking about. It was Pontius Pilate, the Roman governor. He ruled over Judaea, the southern part of the land of Israel. He had decided to build an aqueduct, a high bridge, set up on towers, to carry water. His aqueduct was to bring water to Jerusalem from the reservoirs at Bethlehem, $6\frac{1}{2}$ miles away. Jews were very angry because he took money from the treasury of their Temple to help pay for it. So they were even more delighted when he ran out of money, and had to abandon his great building scheme. How they mocked at him, and laughed at his folly.

Pilate had not counted the cost, and he had to give up. Some people who sought God's kingdom were like that. At first they were keen and full of enthusiasm. Then they found that its demands were too much for them, and they had to give up.

Counting the cost of following Jesus

One day, a rich young ruler came and knelt before Jesus.

'Good master,' he said. 'What must I do to enter the kingdom of God?'

Jesus answered him: 'You know the commandments of the sacred law.'

'Yes, Teacher,' he replied. 'I have lived by them since I was a boy.'

Jesus saw what a fine young man he was, and how good a disciple he would be. But first he must count the cost.

'There is one more thing you must do,' Jesus said to him. 'Sell all you possess, and give the money to the poor. Then your treasure will be in heaven. Then come and follow me.'

The young man's face fell. How could he give up his fine house, his lands, and all his rich possessions?

He got up slowly from his knees, and turned away sadly. The cost of the kingdom, for him, was the one thing that he could not give up.

Jesus watched him go. Then he turned to his disciples. 'How hard it is for those who have riches to enter God's kingdom,' he said. 'It's easier for a camel to go through the eye of a needle.'

The disciples were astonished.

'Who can be saved, then?' they asked.

'All things are possible with God,' Jesus said.

Another man came to Jesus, full of enthusiasm. 'Lord, I will follow you wherever you go!' he cried.

Jesus said to him, 'Foxes have their holes. Birds have their nests. I have nowhere even to lay my head. Can you give up everything for the kingdom of God?'

'I'll follow you, master!' said another man. 'Just let me go home to say goodbye to my family.'

'A good ploughman never looks back,' said Jesus. 'If he does, his furrow is crooked. No one who looks back is fit for the kingdom of God.'

Pure in heart

IN THE SACRED LAWS of the Jews there are many rules about cleanliness. They are concerned with keeping a clean body, eating clean food, and keeping good health. Jews have always kept these rules of health and hygiene, for they are part of their religion. That is why Jews have always been known for good health and hygiene, when people around them suffered from sickness and plague. But there were many rules and customs for another kind of cleanliness, in the time of Jesus. They were strictly kept by priests, and by the pious men called Pharisees. They believed that men must be pure within, before they were fit to enter the presence of God in worship. They could be defiled, and made impure, in many ways. Then they needed special ceremonies of washing to make them pure again. These customs were not for the sake of health or hygiene. They were religious symbols of cleansing themselves within.

'How foolish this is,' said Jesus. 'God sees into your hearts. He judges men by what they are within. It is not things from outside which make you impure and unclean. Evil comes from within, not from outside. Evil desires in your hearts make you unclean. Evil thoughts make you impure. Cleanse yourselves within. It is the pure in heart who enter the kingdom of God.'

You are judged by your hearts
Jesus put his own teachings in place of old laws and the old customs of his people.

'The old law commanded you not to kill. It orders that if you kill anyone you must be judged, and pay the penalty. But I say to you that you are judged by your inner thoughts and desires. Killing comes from anger – you are condemned by the anger in your heart.'

When men made an agreement together it was the custom to seal it with promises and solemn oaths. Bigger promises and more solemn oaths would make sure that the agreement was kept. Men used the name of God, calling on him as witness to the oaths they swore. Jesus condemned these customs.

'The old law told you to keep your promises and to perform your oaths. But I say to you – do not swear oaths at all. It is all the same, whether you swear by God's name, or by heaven, or by earth, or by Jerusalem. For they all belong to God. All you need to say is "Yes" and "No". For if your words are truthful they do not need to be strengthened by promises and oaths. Anything more is evil, for it comes from not speaking truth and not trusting.'

God sees into your hearts
Pharisees were devout men, looked up to by the common people for their devotion to religion. They were not priests, but they lived by the sacred law, keeping it strictly in every detail. This, they believed, made them right with God. Some Pharisees, it seems, became proud of their righteousness. Jesus condemned them as hypocrites, that is, play-actors. They were acting a part in performing their fine religious acts.

One of these was alms-giving, giving money to God and to the needy, to show love for God and compassion for the poor.

'See how these Pharisees give alms,' said Jesus. 'They like everyone to be watching when they put money in the treasury of the Temple, or make gifts to beggars in the street. They might just as well have a trumpet blown, so that everyone will look. They do not give alms for love of God. They do it to win the praise of men. Well, they have the reward they want.

'Do not be hypocrites like them. When you give alms do it secretly. Don't even let one hand know what the other is doing. Your Father sees in secret – he will bless you.'

It was a common custom for men to stand for praying, and to stretch out their arms, raising both hands and eyes to heaven above.

'Look how these Pharisees say their prayers,' said

Jesus to his disciples. 'They stand out, in the synagogues and at street corners, so that everyone can see them. People praise them for their piety – so they get the reward they want. When you pray, do it secretly, where no one can see you. Your Father sees in secret – he will hear you, and answer your prayers.'

Another custom in religion was fasting – going without food. It was done to please God, and win his pity; to show sorrow for sin, and turn away God's anger; to strengthen the soul; and to discipline the body.

Strict fasting included signs of sorrow for sin – going without washing; placing ashes on the head, instead of anointing the head with oil; wearing rough sackcloth. Monday and Thursday in each week were set aside as fasting days. Pharisees kept both days – and sometimes other days too. They used signs of sorrow, too, so that others could see that they were fasting.

'See how these Pharisees fast,' said Jesus. 'They make sure that everyone can tell they are fasting. They win the praise of men for being so religious – and that is the reward they want. When you fast, wash your face, and anoint your head, so that no one knows. Your Father sees in secret – he will reward you.'

Jesus condemned the pride of Pharisees, too.

'They love the place of honor at feasts, and the chief seats in the synagogues. They love to have people bow to them and call them by fine titles. But they are blind guides, leading men astray, and laying heavy burdens on them. Their religion is insincere, for their hearts are proud and loveless. They are like a woman washing-up, cleaning the outside of the cup, but leaving it dirty inside. Unless your righteousness is greater than theirs you cannot enter the kingdom. For only the pure in heart see God.'

Citizens of God's kingdom

Jesus gave a picture of citizens of the kingdom of God:

'Happy are those who wait upon God. They seem unimportant to men, for they do not seek riches or power. They seek after God – their treasure is in heaven. God's kingdom belongs to them.

'Happy are those who grieve over evil and suffering in the world. They long for the coming of God's kingdom. God will comfort them.

'Happy are the humble. They are not proud, for they see themselves as God sees them. But they are strong, for their trust is in God. They will inherit the earth.

'Happy are those who hunger and thirst for the righteousness of God to be seen on earth. They will be satisfied.

'Happy are those who show mercy, who are tenderhearted and forgiving. They will receive God's mercy.

'Happy are those whose hearts are pure and whole, because they are filled with love for God and man. They will see God.

'Happy are those who make peace. They share in God's work. They are his true children.

'Happy are those who suffer for the sake of righteousness. They will be rewarded with the kingdom of God.

'Happy are you, my disciples, when you suffer for my sake. Men will mock you, ill-treat you, and speak evil of you – just as they persecuted the prophets of old. Rejoice when that happens, for your reward will be great in heaven.'

Building the house of character

Jesus had helped to build houses when he worked as a carpenter at Nazareth. When a new house was being built he fitted window frames and doors, and beams for the roof. One of his parables was about this work of building a house which he knew so well.

There were two men, Simon and Jude, who each decided to build a house in a certain valley. They both set to work at about the same time.

Simon was a wise man. He knew that the most important part of any building is the foundation. It must be strong and sure, if a house is to stand firm. So he went on digging down into the earth until he came to solid rock. This was the foundation that he wanted – now he could begin to build his house. For cement he used a strong mortar made of clay, shells, and pieces of broken pottery ground into powder. Slowly but surely his house rose up on the rock. At last it was finished. Simon knew that it was a good, strong house. For, though no one could see its foundation, he knew that it was solid rock.

Jude was very different. He wanted a fine house, and he wanted to build it quickly. He was a foolish man, for he did not bother about a foundation. He built his house on sand. His house rose quickly and he must have felt pleased with himself, for Simon's house was taking much longer. Jude easily finished first. He was proud of his fine-looking house.

In the autumn came the heavy rains of October. There is plenty of rain, in both autumn and spring, in the land of Israel. But it falls in a very few days, in violent storms. The rain was soon teeming down into the valley where the new houses stood. The dried-up wadi, or river-bed, quickly became a raging torrent, swirling round the houses. The gale hurled itself against them. Simon's house, with its rock foundation, stood firm. Neither floods nor storms could harm it. But Jude's house was built on sand. The floods sucked away the sands beneath it, and the storms battered its walls. Soon it began to totter and crumble, till it fell with a resounding crash into the floods and was carried away.

Everyone is building his own house – we call it his character. The wise man, said Jesus, listened to his teaching and followed it in his life. His character was built on rock, a sure foundation. Nothing could break it. The foolish man listened to his words but did not follow them. His character was built on shifting sands – it had no foundation. When the storms of life came he could not stand upright. He was easily carried away.

What was the sure foundation on which the wise man built his character? It was loving God, with all his being, **and loving his neighbor as himself. Happy are those** who build on this foundation. They are the pure in heart. Theirs is the kingdom of heaven.

Jesus the Savior

JESUS WAS ABOUT 30 YEARS OLD when he began his work for God, ministering to the people. His ministry lasted for about three years. He spent most of this time in Galilee, his homeland. Maps often make it seem a big country. But it is really quite small. Jesus made the town of Capernaum the center of his ministry, staying there at the house of Simon Peter the apostle. All the places which Jesus visited in Galilee were within 18 miles of Capernaum.

Jesus went through the countryside, with his group of disciples, on foot. They walked from one town or village to the next. But four of his twelve apostles were fishermen. Their boats were very useful for crossing the Sea of Galilee, to get from one place to another – or even to get away from the crowds which followed Jesus everywhere.

For the fame of Jesus grew, during his journeys in Galilee, and he became a popular prophet. He announced the coming of the kingdom of God, foretold by the prophets of old, and heralded by John the Baptist. He showed the power of God's kingdom in his words and in his deeds.

The teaching of Jesus

The people of Galilee enjoyed listening to Jesus. For his

teaching was fresh and new. It was not like the dry-as-dust teaching of the Scribes, who were experts in the law of God. Nor was it like the teaching of the Rabbis, who taught people how to follow the sacred law in their daily lives.

Jesus drew lessons from common things which the people could see all around them.

'Look at that sower, up there on the hillside, scattering his seed. Watch where it falls . . .'

'Look at that flock of birds, wheeling in the sky. God provides food for them. How much more will he care for you! So do not worry about food and clothes . . .'

'Look at the carpet of spring flowers under your feet, lovely lilies and anemones. It is God who clothes the wild flowers in all their beauty. Will he not much more clothe you? . . .'

Jesus taught the people in stories, not in sermons. His stories began: 'The kingdom of God is like . . .'. That is why his stories are called 'parables' which means 'comparisons', comparing one thing with another. For Jesus likened the kingdom of God to everyday things – to happenings in nature, to happenings in the world of men. His stories were about life on earth, but they taught about life with God. They used everyday life to teach about life in the kingdom of God.

Jesus used picture sayings, as well as picture stories. He said to his disciples, 'You are to be the light of the world.' The oil lamp, used to give light in the home, was not hidden away. It was put out in the open, on a stand, so that everyone could see its light. The disciples were to let their light shine openly in the world, so that men would see the glory of God.

Jesus also said to his disciples, 'You are to be the salt of the earth.' Salt was very precious, especially in a hot country, where food quickly went bad without salt to preserve it. People could not live without salt. It kept food fresh and pure. The disciples were to be like that – the 'salt' of the world of men.

There was one thing about the teaching of Jesus which struck everyone. He spoke with authority.

Jesus did not begin, 'The Rabbis say . . .'. He began, 'I say unto you . . .'. It seemed as if he spoke directly from God.

Sometimes Jesus put his teaching in the place of the sacred law of his people. 'You remember that the old law said . . . But I say unto you . . .' It seemed that he was bringing a new law from God.

Who was Jesus, the people wondered. Who was this prophet who spoke directly from God; who gave his own teaching, not that of the Rabbis; who even put his own

teaching in place of the sacred law of God?

Jesus forgives sins

Jesus showed the power of God's kingdom in his deeds, as well as in his words.

One day Jesus was in Peter's house in Capernaum. Soon people heard that he was there, the news quickly spread, and a crowd gathered. They filled the house, right to the door, and others were standing outside, craning their necks to try to see Jesus.

Now it happened that four men came, bringing a sick friend. For they were sure that Jesus could heal him, if only they could get to the prophet. They carried their friend on a thin mattress, for he was paralyzed and could not move any part of his body. When they saw the crowd there seemed no hope of getting to Jesus.

But they were quite determined to reach Jesus. They carried their friend up the stone stairway, on the outside of the house, which led up to the flat roof. The roof was made by strong wooden beams, laid across the tops of the walls. The beams were filled in with brushwood, and branches, and mud, making them firm and flat. It did not take the four men long to make a hole in the roof. Soon it was big enough for the mattress to go through, and they let their friend down till he lay at the feet of Jesus.

Jesus admired the faith of the four men. He said to the paralyzed man, 'My son, your sins are forgiven you.'

Now some Scribes were sitting there in the crowd, curious to find out about this new prophet. They were horrified at his words.

'Who does this man think he is?' they murmured. 'Only God can forgive sins. This is blasphemy!'

Jesus knew what they were thinking. 'What are you worried about?' he said to the Scribes. 'Which is easier — to say to this paralyzed man, "Your sins are forgiven," or to say, "Get up, take your mattress, and walk."? You must know that the Son of Man has power to forgive sins.' Then he said to the man, 'I say to you, stand up, take your mattress, and go home.'

Then the man who had been paralyzed stood up. He rolled his thin mattress under his arm, and walked out in front of everyone.

'We never saw anything like this!' the people said to each other in amazement.

Jesus would not argue with the Scribes about himself. He simply called himself 'Son of Man'. What did he mean?

Savior – Messiah – Christ

Jesus had known from the beginning that he was the Savior, foretold by the prophets of old. They had told how, when the Savior came, he would set up God's kingdom on earth. So Jews looked forward to the coming of the Savior. They called him the Messiah, that is, the Anointed One. For, just as Jewish kings were anointed, the Messiah would be anointed by God to rule over his heavenly kingdom. In the language of the Greeks the word for the Anointed One was 'Christ'. That is why followers of Jesus call him Jesus Christ. For they believe in Jesus as the Christ, the Anointed One of God.

While the Jews waited for the coming of the Messiah they had suffered terribly, as a people. They were conquered by one kingdom after another. How they longed to be free! Their hopes of the Savior changed. They longed for a Messiah who would show himself by great signs and wonders. He would turn stones into bread, and fill them with plenty. He would come down to earth on the clouds of heaven, and perform great miracles. He would use his powers to drive out the Romans, and to give his people a kingdom – perhaps even an empire.

Jesus had faced these temptations before he began his ministry. He had conquered them, and rejected them. He would not be the kind of Messiah that the people wanted. That was why he did not call himself the Messiah.

Jesus called himself 'Son of Man' instead. It was a strange title for the Messiah, and few people would understand it. To Jesus it meant the kind of Savior described in the book of Isaiah the prophet, one who would be the 'suffering servant' of God. He would seek to win men to God by love alone. He would be unpopular, not giving people what they wanted. He would be cast out, rejected, and done to death. But he would show men the love of God both in his living and in his dying. And God would raise him up to glory.

How hard it was for people to understand that kind of Messiah.

Jesus is not the popular Messiah

Once a big crowd of people got very excited. There seemed to be thousands of them. They had followed Jesus out into the hill-country, and there he taught them. When it grew late, his disciples came to him anxiously.

'This is a lonely place and it's getting late,' they said to Jesus. 'Send the people away so that they can get food.'

'You give them something to eat,' Jesus said to Philip, who looked after getting food for the disciples.

'We'd need a great deal of money to buy enough food for all these people,' said Philip.

'How many loaves have you? Go and see,' Jesus replied.

96

Andrew came up and said, 'There's a boy here, with food in his satchel. He's got five small barley loaves and two small fishes. But what's the use of them with a crowd like this?'

'Tell the people to sit down,' Jesus told the disciples.

The apostle Simon Peter never forgot that day. He described it to Mark who wrote it down in his Gospel in Peter's own words. Peter remembered how the people were wearing bright clothes. When they sat down, in groups, they looked just like colorful flower-beds in a neat garden, with green grass between each group.

Jesus took the five loaves and two fishes, offered by the boy. He looked up to heaven in prayer, blessed the food, and broke the flat loaves of brown barley bread into pieces. He gave them to the disciples to share among the people. He did the same with the fishes. All the people ate and were filled. And the disciples filled twelve baskets with the pieces of food left over.

We are not told any more about what happened that evening. But we do know what happened after the feeding. The crowd became very excited. It seems that they remembered one of the prophecies of the Messiah. When the Messiah came, it was written, he would feed the people in a great banquet. The people jumped up, and shouted aloud in excitement. 'The Messiah!' they cried. 'Crown him! Crown him!'

They ran toward Jesus to make him king by force. But he must not be taken as the Messiah they wanted. Some think that, in the gathering dusk, he changed his cloak for the cloak of a disciple, and so passed through the crowd unrecognized. He left his disciples there, and went away into the hills alone.

Jesus was the Anointed One. But he was not the Messiah whom the people expected. It was hard for them to understand. It was hard for his own apostles, too.

Jesus the Christ

 T FIRST, Jesus was a popular prophet in
Galilee, and crowds gathered round him
wherever he went. He proclaimed the coming
of the kingdom of God among men. He
showed the power of God's love in his words
and in his deeds. The common people heard him gladly –
though Jesus knew that much of the seed he was sowing
among them would be wasted. But it was not like that
with the religious leaders of the people, the Scribes and
Pharisees. The more popular Jesus became the more
suspicious they grew. Scribes were experts in the sacred
writings of the law and of the prophets. Pharisees lived
strictly by the written law, and kept every detail of it in
their daily lives. They also kept the 'unwritten law' –
rules and customs and beliefs which had grown up, and
which were just as sacred to them.

Jesus spoke against Scribes and Pharisees. He called
them hypocrites, that is, play-actors. For to him their
religion was an outward show. He condemned their pious
customs, like fasting and washing. He broke their sacred
rules for the sabbath in order to help those in need. He
put his own teachings in place of the sacred law. He
made friends with sinners who were condemned and
made outcasts by their religion. He criticized Scribes and
Pharisees openly, so that they were in danger of losing

the respect of the people.

Scribes and Pharisees looked down on the people of Galilee, in the north. Most of them lived in Judaea in the south, especially in the holy city of Jerusalem. There, too, lived the leaders of the people called Sadducees. They were the Chief Priests and rich nobles who controlled the Temple and its worship. They were the leaders of the Council of the Jews – a law-court which the Romans allowed to look after Jewish affairs. Sadducees were on good terms with the Roman rulers, so that their power and wealth were safe. Galilee was a trouble-spot to them. For sometimes a revolt against the Romans broke out in Galilee, led by someone claiming to be the promised Messiah. Sadducees were suspicious when they heard about Jesus, the new prophet in Galilee.

Enemies in Galilee

In Galilee, too, Jesus had enemies. They were the Herodians, the followers of King Herod who ruled over Galilee. Herod was sly and suspicious, cunning as a fox. He was superstitious – ready to believe anything. He had put John the Baptist to death. When he heard about Jesus, the new prophet, he was afraid that it might be John the Baptist come back from the dead. Herod knew that he was hated by the people of Galilee. So he was afraid of anyone who was popular among them. That was why he wanted to get hold of Jesus.

Jesus knew that he was in danger of being arrested by Herod's men. He crossed the borders of Galilee into the land of the Phoenicians with his disciples. There they were out of Herod's reach – and away from the constant crowds, too.

When they returned to Galilee there were Pharisees and Sadducees waiting for Jesus. He crossed the Sea of Galilee with his disciples, in their fishing boats, and landed on the other side. They were safe there, too. For they were in the territory ruled over by Philip, the brother of Herod, but a far finer ruler.

Jesus and his disciples set out on foot to the north, climbing the hills toward the mighty Mount Hermon. It soars up nearly 9,900 feet above sea level. It is so high that its peak is covered with snow all the year round. Its melting snows give birth to the river Jordan. The river begins in a cave, which had been sacred to Pan, a god of the Greeks. The town which grew up there was named Pan's Place. King Philip had rebuilt the town and given it a new name – Caesarea. But there was another town named Caesarea, which lay by the Mediterranean Sea in the land of Israel. So Philip's new town became known as Philip's Caesarea – it was called Caesarea Philippi.

Jesus is the Christ

Jesus and his disciples were quite unknown at Caesarea Philippi. So they found peace and quiet among the foreigners who lived there. It was here that Jesus spoke to his disciples about himself.

'Who do men say that I am?' he asked them.

They told Jesus the different beliefs which people had about him.

'Some say that you are John the Baptist, come back to life.'

'Some say that you are Elijah, the prophet who would come again.'

'Some say that you are Jeremiah, or one of the other great prophets.'

'But who do you say that I am?' Jesus asked them, directly, for the very first time. They had been with him for a long time now – time enough to have made up their minds about him.

It was bluff, forthright Peter who blurted it out.

'We believe that you are the Christ, the promised Messiah.'

'God has blessed you, Simon,' said Jesus. 'For no man has made this known to you. It has been revealed to you by my Father in heaven.'

Jesus was glad that his apostles had come to believe in him. For now he could speak to them openly – and prepare them for what must come to pass. But it was to be a secret among them. Jesus strictly ordered them to tell no one that he was the Christ. People must not think of him as the kind of Messiah they wanted.

The Christ must suffer

Now Jesus began to prepare his apostles for the future. He knew what must come. He was the suffering servant, foretold by the prophet – the one who would love to the utmost, and be faithful to the bitter end. Now he told his apostles. He must go to Jerusalem, when his time came. There he would be rejected, and suffer, and die, and be raised up by God.

The apostles were horrified. They looked forward to sharing with Jesus in the glory of God's kingdom – and here he was, talking about being rejected, and suffering, and dying!

Again it was Simon Peter who bluntly spoke out. 'God forbid it, Lord!' he cried. 'This shall never happen to you!'

Jesus turned upon him sternly. 'Get behind me, you tempter! The evil one speaks through you! You are a hindrance to me when you say such things!'

Simon Peter was speaking like the tempter of old. Long ago, before Jesus had started his ministry, he had fought a hard battle against the evil one. He had conquered the temptation to take the easy way, to be the kind of Messiah the people wanted. He must follow God's way, the way of love, the way that meant being rejected, and suffering, and dying, to win men to God.

The vision at Mount Hermon

After some days, in the quiet hills, Jesus called to him his three closest apostles, Peter and James and John. They climbed the foothills of Mount Hermon. Jesus went some way ahead of them to pray. And suddenly, looking up towards him, they saw Jesus against the sheer snow-white of the mountain. His face seemed to shine like the sun. His garments glistened with light, as no cleaner on earth could have whitened them. It seemed, too, that Jesus was not alone – that with him were Moses, the law-giver, and Elijah, the great prophet.

The three apostles were terrified. Peter blurted out, 'Lord, it is good for us to be here! We can make three tabernacles – for you, and Moses, and Elijah!'

It was all he could think of saying. After all, it was the time of the Feast of Tabernacles, the harvest festival of Jews. At this feast they set up tabernacles – shady tents or booths, made with leafy branches – just as their ancestors had done during their wanderings with Moses. So they would be keeping the feast properly, if the three of them made tabernacles. Besides, one of the lessons for the feast, read in the synagogue, told how Moses had gone up the mountain and there beheld the glory of God, so that his face shone.

But, hardly had Peter spoken, than the dazzling cloud of God's glory overshadowed Jesus, and from it came a voice: 'This is my beloved son.' The three apostles, blinded by the vision, and stricken with awe, fell on their faces. And when they dared to look up again they saw only Jesus coming toward them.

'Tell no one what you have seen, until the Son of Man is risen from the dead,' he said to them.

They dared not ask what he meant.

On the road to Jerusalem

THE STORY OF THE MINISTRY of Jesus is told in the Bible in four Gospels – that is, books of Good News. The three Gospels of Matthew and Mark and Luke tell of the ministry of Jesus in Galilee. They record only two visits made by Jesus to Jerusalem – the first when he was a boy, and the second when he went to the holy city to suffer and to die. It is likely that Jesus went to Jerusalem more often. It was the religious duty of every Jewish man to go to the holy city as a pilgrim, to worship in the Temple at the great feasts. Jews living in the land of Israel would be able to attend regularly. Jews living in other lands travelled to Jerusalem, when they could — especially for the Passover, the greatest feast of the whole year.

The fourth Gospel, the Gospel of John, tells of the ministry of Jesus in Judaea and how, during that time, he made other visits to Jerusalem. He went to the Temple for the Feast of Tabernacles in October, and for the Feast of Lights in December. But he did not go about openly. For there were plots against him in Jerusalem. News of the words and deeds of Jesus spread far and wide. Leaders of the Sadducees and the Pharisees met together in the Council.

'What are we to do?' they said. 'If we let him go on

like this everyone will believe in him and follow him. Then the Romans will suspect another rebellion against them. They will take away all power from us and rule the country for themselves. They will destroy our nation, and our holy Temple.'

Caiaphas, the High Priest, gave his decision. 'We cannot allow our nation to perish,' he said. 'We can only save our people by getting rid of this Jesus. It is fitting that one man should die in order that the people may live.'

When Jesus was in Galilee he had avoided arrest by King Herod. Now, in Judaea, he avoided arrest by the leaders of the Council. He was not running away. He was waiting for the right time – the time when he would make his open claim to be the promised Savior. It had to be in the most sacred place – the Holy City of Jerusalem. It had to be at the most sacred time – the Feast of Passover.

The Son of Man must suffer

One day, Jesus was walking with his twelve apostles. They came to a crossroads. It was where the road to Jerusalem was joined by a path leading to the hills – and to safety. Jesus, walking ahead, took the road to Jerusalem. The twelve, following at a distance, were horrified to see Jesus walking into danger. They stopped at the crossroads. Jesus, looking round and seeing them there, had to come back. Only as he came near could they see how grievously troubled he was. He spoke to them urgently.

'We are going up to Jerusalem. The Son of Man will be delivered to the Chief Priests and Scribes. They will sentence him to death, and hand him over to the Romans. They will mock him, spit on him, scourge him, and kill him. After three days he will rise.'

Jesus had spoken before about the suffering which awaited him in Jerusalem. But the apostles could not give up their hope of glory in the kingdom of God. If Jesus must suffer they would stand by him, and share whatever happened. But the suffering would not last long. And then would come the triumph of Jesus, and their share in his glory. James and John, who were always close to Jesus, thought like this. They wanted to be sure. So, after Jesus had spoken of his suffering, they asked him, 'Master, will you do whatever we ask?'

'What do you want me to do for you?' said Jesus.

'Grant that we two may sit with you when you reign in glory, one on your right hand, and one on your left.'

'You do not know what you are asking,' Jesus sighed. 'I have to pass through deep waters of suffering. Can you share in my suffering?'

'We can, Master.'

'You will indeed share in it,' Jesus said. 'But places of honor in my Father's kingdom are not for me to grant. They are prepared for others.'

The rest of the apostles were angry at the request of James and John. Jesus spoke to all of them: 'You know that in earthly kingdoms there are kings and rulers. They have power and authority to lord it over others. It must not be like that among you. Whoever wants to be great among you must be your servant. Whoever wants to be first must be the slave of all. For the Son of Man came, not to rule, but to serve. He has come to die for others, to pay the price of bringing men back to God.'

Mary's loving deed

Jesus and his band of disciples passed through Jericho on their way to Jerusalem. With them on the road were crowds of pilgrims, going to the holy city for the great Passover feast. It was just like it had been when Jesus, as a boy of twelve, had taken this same road on his very first visit to Jerusalem.

They came to Bethany, a village almost 2 miles outside Jerusalem. There lived a family who had long been friends of Jesus – Mary and Martha, and their brother Lazarus. Jesus had often stayed with them, and this would be his home during the Passover.

Martha was a busy housewife. She was soon bustling round, preparing a fine supper for Jesus and his apostles. Mary showed her devotion to Jesus in a different way. She loved to sit at his feet, listening to his words, filled with the beauty of his teaching. But for this supper she had planned something very special. Perhaps she had sensed the danger that awaited Jesus.

It was the custom for guests invited to a house to have their feet washed from the dust of the road, and to have their heads anointed with cool and refreshing oil. Mary wanted to show her great love for Jesus. She had a rare and costly gift for him. It was a tiny phial, made of white alabaster, and shaped like a little jug. It contained just a few drops of a precious oil called spikenard, brought by ship and camel from faraway India.

Mary broke off the narrow neck of the tiny flask to open it. Then she let the drops of precious perfume fall on to the head of Jesus. At once the whole house was filled with its fragrance.

Judas Iscariot, one of the apostles, was horrified. He looked after the money for Jesus and his disciples, and that was how he judged Mary's loving act.

'What a waste!' he said indignantly. 'That oil could have been sold for $7,500 and the money shared among the poor.'

104

Others thought the same, and they criticized Mary too.

'Let her alone!' said Jesus. 'Why do you trouble her? She has done something beautiful to show her devotion. There are always poor people around you. You can help them whenever you want. But you will not always have me with you. Mary has done what she could. It is as if she knew I was going to die, and was anointing my body before the burial.

'Truly, I tell you, her loving deed will never be forgotten.'

The stage is set at Jerusalem

It was now six days before the Passover. The feast came at the beginning of April, and it lasted for eight days. Jews came to the holy city from all over the land of Israel, and from their homes in other lands. The city was packed with pilgrims. Many people camped outside Jerusalem. Others, like Jesus and his apostles, lodged in nearby villages.

To Jerusalem, too, came Pontius Pilate, the Roman governor of Judaea. His headquarters were at Caesarea, a fine town by the Mediterranean Sea. He made sure of being in Jerusalem during the Jewish feasts. For all kinds of trouble could break out in the crowded and excited city. He must be on the spot to deal with any threat to law and order.

Pilate may have had another reason, too. It was a custom at the feast for the governor to release prisoners, as a special act of mercy. He knew how often he had offended the Jews by his decisions. If he were there, and kept the custom, it might make him more popular with the Jews.

Now the stage was set for Jesus to come to the Holy City as Savior.

Jesus enters Jerusalem

T
HE LAST WEEK in the earthly life of Jesus is called Holy Week by Christians. It began with the day called Palm Sunday, the day when Jesus entered Jerusalem. Jesus had come to Jerusalem in good time for the Passover Feast. He was staying at the village of Bethany, almost 2 miles outside the city, with his friends Mary and Martha, and their brother Lazarus. On the first day of the week, our Sunday, Jesus sent two disciples on to the village of Bethphage, a little over half a mile from Jerusalem.

'As you come into the village you will see an ass, tethered to railings beside the road,' Jesus told them. 'Untie the ass and bring it to me. If anyone asks what you are doing just say, "The Master needs it, and he will send it back immediately after."'

When the two disciples reached Bethphage it was exactly as Jesus had told them, for Jesus was borrowing the ass from a friend, and he would understand.

Why did Jesus want the ass? Asses, of course, were common beasts of burden in those days. They carried great loads, as well as their owners. They could pick their way through crowded streets. They were sure-footed, going uphill or downhill.

But these were not the reasons why Jesus chose to enter the holy city riding upon an ass. He was openly and deliberately fulfilling one of the prophecies of the promised Savior: 'Behold, O Jerusalem! Your king is coming to you humbly, riding upon an ass.'

Kings rode on horses, and so did soldiers. Horses were symbols of power, and of war. But there was nothing proud or warlike about an ass. It was a symbol of humility, and of peace. Jesus did not seek out a horse, to fulfil the prophecy of a king. He rode into Jerusalem humbly on an ass.

The disciples threw cloaks over the ass, to make a saddle, and set Jesus upon it. The ass picked its way down the hill, across the valley of the brook called Kidron, and up the steep climb to the city walls of Jerusalem. Jesus was escorted by his own disciples. There were many other pilgrims from Galilee, on the road. They soon recognized Jesus and began shouting to greet him. Soon there was an excited and joyful crowd around him. Some cut down leafy branches from the palm trees to wave in his honor. Others spread garments in the road to make a royal way for him. There were many shouts of 'Hosanna!' – the cry of joy and praise used in religious processions. Soon the crowd were singing in chorus the verse of the hymn they knew so well: 'Hosanna! Blessed is he who comes in the name of the Lord!'

It was a happy and joyous little procession of pilgrims from Galilee. But there were Pharisees standing by the road who were disgusted by the noisy and disorderly crowd.

'Master, tell your disciples to behave themselves properly!' they said to Jesus indignantly.

'I tell you that if they remained silent the very stones would cry out!' Jesus answered them.

So Jesus entered the holy city, and beheld the Temple glittering in all its glory of gold and white marble. And his eyes filled with tears, and his heart with sorrow, as he foresaw the fate which must surely come to Jerusalem.

'O Jerusalem, Jerusalem,' he wept over the city. 'If only you knew, even now, where you might find your peace! How often I would have gathered your people together, as a hen gathers her chicks under the safety of her wings! But you would not let me!'

Jesus cleanses the Temple

Jesus and his disciples went back to the peace and safety of Bethany for the night. The next day, Monday, he came back to the holy city. Now for a second time, openly and deliberately, he fulfilled a prophecy of the promised Savior.

Jesus went into the large Outer Court of the Temple.

107

It was much less sacred than the Inner Courts of the Temple. Even foreigners and pagans were allowed into it. But a large notice was posted there, written in the languages of both Greeks and Romans. It warned them, on pain of death, not to go any nearer to the holy Temple of the God of the Jews.

The Outer Court had become like a market-place. Some people used it simply as a short cut. There were many stalls there for traders who sold animals used in sacrifice at the Temple. Their stalls were laden with crates of doves, while sheep and oxen were kept nearby. Every family needed a lamb to sacrifice at the Passover feast.

In the Outer Court, too, were spread out the tables of the money-changers, the bankers of those times. For many different kinds of money were used in the land of Israel. Money-changers were specially needed at the Temple. For devout Jews came to Jerusalem for the Passover feast from many lands, bringing the foreign money which they used. They would have Greek money, Roman money, or coins minted by local rulers in Egypt or Asia Minor. No foreign money could be used for paying religious dues at the Temple, so all these coins had to be changed. Only 'holy shekels' could be used. They were coins called 'staters', which came originally from Tyre, the great trading city of Phoenicia, by the Mediterranean Sea. The stater was holy because it was equal to the old Jewish coin called a shekel. Every Jew had to pay the Temple tax of half a shekel at Passover time. So everyone needed to use the money-changers. They were licensed by the priests, so that they made money for the Temple, as well as for themselves.

It was into this noisy, bustling market-place that Jesus came, on that Monday in Holy Week. He had seen it all before. He must have been horrified by it then, too. But it was now that he acted, calmly and deliberately. He took hold of the tables of the money-changers and over-turned them, one by one, so that their careful piles of coins crashed to the pavement, ringing on the flag-stones, scattering far and wide. Then he picked up pieces of rope, tied them together to make a whip, and drove out the sheep and oxen, turning the Outer Court into wild confusion.

'Take these things away!' Jesus cried aloud. 'This is God's house, a house of prayer! You have turned it into a den of thieves!'

Jesus was not losing his temper. This was not 'righteous indignation' as it is called when someone is angry at seeing evil, or wrongdoing, or injustice. Jesus was fulfilling another prophecy of the promised Savior:

'The Lord whom ye seek shall suddenly come to his Temple, and purify it,' said the prophet of old.

Jesus, for the second time, was openly and deliberately and calmly claiming to be the promised Savior.

The parable of wicked husbandmen

The next day, Tuesday, Jesus came again to the Temple. He spoke to the people in one of the inner, most sacred courts. Priests and Scribes were there, trying to catch Jesus out. He told them a parable.

A certain man planted a vineyard, he had the ground thoroughly prepared, and good vines planted. He had a hedge planted around the vineyard, a pit dug for the winepress, and a watch-tower set up for guarding it. Now it was finished. But now he had to travel to a foreign country. So he let his vineyard out to tenants. These husbandmen agreed to pay their rent when grape-harvest came round.

When it was harvest-time the owner sent one of his servants to collect his rent. But the husbandmen had no intention of paying. They beat the owner's servant and sent him off with nothing.

The owner sent another of his servants for the rent. When the wicked husbandmen saw him coming they threw stones at him, wounding his head, and then pushed him out of the vineyard.

The owner sent other servants to collect his rent. Some were beaten, and others were killed, by the evil tenants.

Then the owner decided what must be done. 'I'll send my son, my only son,' he said to himself. 'They will respect him.'

The wicked husbandmen saw the owner's son coming into the vineyard. 'It's the owner's son!' they cried. 'He's the heir to the vineyard! Kill him and we shall inherit it!'

So they killed the only son of the owner of the vineyard, and cast his body outside.

'What will the owner do now?' said Jesus. 'He will come and punish those wicked husbandmen. He will cast them out of his vineyard, and give it to others.'

Everyone in the crowd knew what Jesus meant. A vineyard had always been a symbol for Israel. The husbandmen were the chosen people of God. He had sent prophets, one by one, to his people. Their leaders had ill-treated his prophets, rejected them, killed them. Now he had sent his only son. He too would be rejected and killed.

The priests and Scribes were furious when they heard this parable told against them. They would have seized

Jesus there and then, but for the crowd whom they feared. They stalked off angrily to plot together against him.

Is it right to pay Roman taxes?

Later came Pharisees and Herodians. They had thought up a cunning question to trap Jesus. They began with compliments: 'Master, we know that you speak for God. You teach the truth, and you fear no man, however great. Tell us – is it right to pay taxes to the Romans, or not?'

The crowd waited in breathless silence to hear what Jesus would say. It was indeed a cunning question. If Jesus said it was wrong to pay taxes to the Romans the Chief Priests could have him arrested at once, as a rebel against Rome. That would be the end of him. But, of course, everyone hated paying Roman taxes. So if Jesus said it was right to pay them he would anger the crowd. His popularity would be gone. No one would listen to him any more. Then his enemies would be able to arrest him quietly, and get rid of him. It seemed that Jesus was cornered – there was no way out for him.

Jesus was well aware of the trickery of his enemies. 'What hypocrites you are,' he answered. 'Fetch me a Roman denarius.' This was a silver coin, very common in the land of Israel. But someone had to go and fetch one, for no foreign coins were allowed in the sacred courts of the Temple.

Jesus took the coin, and held it out on his hand. The head of the Roman emperor, Caesar, was clearly engraved on it.

'Whose image can you see on this coin?' Jesus asked.

'The image of Caesar,' his enemies replied.

'Give to Caesar what belongs to Caesar. Give to God what belongs to God,' Jesus answered them.

The coin, bearing the image of Caesar, belonged to Caesar. Man, made in the image of God, belongs to God.

The people were amazed by the answers of Jesus to his questioners. But the Pharisees and Herodians went away angry at being made to look foolish in front of the people. They plotted with the Chief Priests and Scribes. For they were all united in wanting to get rid of Jesus. But Jesus was surrounded by people all day long and at night he was not to be found in the city. They dared not risk arresting him in front of the people. That could cause a riot, and an uprising in the crowded city would give the Romans an excuse to clamp down even more upon the Jews.

How could they lay hold of Jesus without any trouble?

Jesus foretells the fall of Jerusalem

As Jesus left the Temple, to return to Bethany for the night, his disciples said, 'Master, look at these great stones, and these marvellous buildings!'

The Temple was indeed a wonderful building. Its walls were made of stones about 11½ feet long and over 3 feet high, some weighing 100 tons.

Jesus answered them sadly. 'I tell you, the time will come when there will not be one stone upon another.'

It was 40 years after the earthly life of Jesus that the Jews made their final revolt against the Romans. Jerusalem was beseiged, captured, and destroyed. Only the Wailing Wall, as devout Jews call it, remains today to show the glory of the Temple that was once the crown of the holy city.

The suffering of Jesus

THE LEADERS OF THE PEOPLE were all agreed that they must get rid of Jesus for he was a threat to all of them. But how could they arrest him, without causing a riot in the crowded and excited city? The answer came in one of his twelve apostles. It was Judas, called Iscariot to distinguish him from the other Judas among them. Judas Iscariot was the only one of the apostles who did not come from Galilee in the north. 'Iscariot' means 'Man of Kerioth', a village of Judaea in the south. But some think it may mean 'Dagger-bearer', the name given to fanatic Jews who made an underground movement against the Romans.

Judas Iscariot looked after the money bag for the disciples. He may have loved money, and was even ready to betray his master for it. But some think that he did not understand Jesus. What he wanted was for Jesus to proclaim himself as the popular Messiah, and to lead the people against the Romans. He would force Jesus to declare himself by getting him arrested. For then Jesus would have to say openly who he was.

Whatever his reason, Judas Iscariot went to the Chief Priests on the Wednesday of that last week. He offered to betray Jesus to them. They could arrest Jesus at any time, of course. So Judas was not important to them. But it would help if they could seize Jesus when he was alone. So they agreed to pay Judas for betraying Jesus to them. One story said that the reward for his treachery was 30 pieces of silver, coins of the Phoenicians, called staters – and the price for buying a slave.

Preparing for the Last Supper

Thursday was the day before the Passover, and it was the time of preparation for the sacred feast.

The Passover celebrates how God had delivered the ancestors of the Jews from slavery in Egypt, and how he had led them out, by Moses, into the Promised Land. The festival began in the home with thorough preparation – cleaning, making new clothes, preparing special foods. The Passover lamb was slain, and part offered in the Temple as sacrifice. The remainder was used for the sacred Passover meal, in which everything had its own special meaning. Bitter herbs stood for the bitter life of slavery in Egypt. Unleavened bread was like that eaten by the Jewish slaves on their hasty flight from Egypt.

Supper, on that Thursday evening, was part of the preparation. The Passover meal, with all its solemn ritual, came on the Friday. But Jesus knew that his time was short. Supper on that Thursday evening would be the Passover meal for Jesus and his disciples.

Jesus sent two disciples to prepare for their Last Supper together. They were to go to the city gate, where they would see a man carrying a pitcher of water and they were to follow him. This was a sign which had been arranged. For it was only women who carried water, in their pitchers – except for the despised men water-carriers with their wineskins.

The house to which the man led them was the house of Mark, who was to write the first Gospel many years later. He was only a boy at this time. His mother was a disciple of Jesus and her house was to become the meeting-place of the first Christian church. For she was rich enough to have a large guest-chamber, built on the flat roof of her house. She had gladly offered it to Jesus for that Last Supper.

We can understand why it was secretly planned. Jesus was going to do something very important at the supper, and he must not be disturbed. Only his most trusted disciples knew where it was to be held. That had to be kept a secret, most of all from Judas Iscariot.

Jesus makes a New Covenant

When evening came, Jesus led his apostles to the house, and they went up the stone stairway outside the house to the upper-room. Everything was ready for them.

It was the custom for servants to wash the hot, dusty feet of guests with water. Jesus himself washed the feet of his apostles. 'I have given you an example,' he said, after he had knelt before each of them in turn. 'You must serve others as I have served you.' During the meal, Jesus took one of the flat, round loaves of bread and blessed it. Then he broke it into pieces, and gave one to each of the apostles.

'Take and eat,' he said. 'This bread is my body, which is given for you. Do this in remembrance of me.'

Then he took the large cup of wine and blessed it. He passed it round for all the apostles to share.

'Drink of this,' he said. 'For this wine is my blood, which is shed for you. Do this in remembrance of me.'

And Jesus said, 'This is the New Covenant. I am making it with my own blood.'

A 'covenant' or 'testament' means a binding together of men with God. The Old Covenant, or Old Testament, had been made between God and his chosen people by Moses. It had been made through the life-blood of an animal sacrifice, which bound the people to God. Later a prophet named Jeremiah had foretold that God would make a New Covenant with men. Jesus was making this New Covenant, or New Testament. It was being made through his own life-blood. He himself was the sacrifice.

Still today, 2,000 years later, Christian followers of Jesus remember him in bread and wine, used in their worship as the body and blood of Jesus given for them. They enter into his New Covenant which binds them to God.

Agony in the Garden of Gethsemane
The Last Supper ended with singing the Passover hymns. Then Jesus led the apostles out through the city gate, in the pale moonlight. As they walked together he said, 'You will all turn against me this night. Even as it is written – "The shepherd will be taken, and the sheep will be scattered."'

At once Peter burst out, 'Even if they all leave you I never will!'

Jesus answered him, 'Truly, I tell you, that this very night, before the cock crows twice, you will deny me three times.'

Peter was even more passionate: 'Even if I must die with you I will not deny you!'

They all said the same.

Young Mark had heard them singing in the upper room, and then going down the stairway. He was very curious and he followed them, wearing only his white linen tunic. Jesus led his apostles over the brook Kidron, and up the slope to the Mount of Olives. He took them into a quiet garden named Gethsemane, that is, Oil-press. For it was there that olives from the trees, higher up the hill, were pressed to make olive-oil.

Judas Iscariot, who had gone out during the Last Supper, knew that this was a favorite place of Jesus.

Jesus took his three closest apostles, Peter and James and John, into a quiet, peaceful part of the garden.

'My soul is full of sorrow,' Jesus said in a broken voice. 'Stay here and keep watch.'

He went a little way from them, and fell to the ground in agony of spirit.

'Abba, Father,' they heard him cry. "All things are possible to you. Take this suffering from me. But let your will be done, not mine.'

The three apostles could not share his agony in the garden. For their eyes were heavy, and sleep overcame them. Twice Jesus came to them and found them sleeping. Then he woke them a third time: 'The hour has come. Rise, and let us go. The Son of Man is betrayed, and the betrayer comes.'

The arrest of Jesus

Now they could see lights flickering among the trees, and hear the growing sound of voices. A band of men armed with swords and clubs was coming toward. them. Now they could make out the leader of the crowd. It was Judas Iscariot.

He came straight up to Jesus.

'Hail, master!' he said out loud, as he gave Jesus the kiss of greeting and friendship.

That was the signal to the servants of the Chief Priests. They ran toward Jesus and his apostles.

Peter snatched a sword and lashed out with it. By chance he slashed the ear of one of the men.

'Stop!' cried Jesus. 'Put away the sword.' And he touched the man's wound with his healing power.

As the men bound the hands of Jesus he said to them, 'Why have you come after me with swords and clubs, as if you were chasing a robber? Day by day I have been teaching in the Temple. You could have seized me there.'

Young Mark had followed them into the garden. He was hiding behind a tree, close at hand. But the white of his tunic gave him away, and one of the men grabbed at him. Mark was terrified, and desperately tried to wriggle out of his tunic which the man was clutching. At last he was free, and he fled naked from the garden.

Mark never forgot that night. When he wrote his Gospel, many years later, he added his own memory to the story of that night in the garden of Gethsemane.

Jesus was led away captive. It had been just as he foretold. The shepherd was taken, and the sheep had scattered.

All his apostles had fled.

115

The death of Jesus

ESUS WAS LED BACK to Jerusalem by the armed men, with his hands bound. They took him first to the house of Annas, the former High Priest, who had great authority. He would decide whether there was enough evidence against Jesus to bring him to trial. He questioned Jesus about his teachings and his followers.

'I have always spoken openly, in synagogues, and in the Temple,' said Jesus. 'I kept nothing secret. Why ask me? Ask those who heard me – they know what I taught.'

An officer standing by struck Jesus with his hand. 'Is that the way to answer the High Priest?' he cried.

'If I have said something wrong, say what my offense is,' said Jesus. 'If I have not spoken wrong why do you strike me?'

Annas sent Jesus on to Caiaphas, his son-in-law, who was High Priest that year. Caiaphas had already given his opinion about Jesus. Jewish leaders had been worried lest the people become so stirred up by Jesus as to riot against the Romans. Then the Romans would enslave the Jews, and take away what freedom they had.

'We cannot allow our nation to perish,' Caiaphas had decided. 'It is fitting that one man should die, so that the whole people may live.'

By now Caiaphas had gathered leaders of the Council at his house, ready to examine Jesus. He had got witnesses, too, who were ready to bring evidence against Jesus. It was a rule of Jewish law that each witness should be heard separately and that their separate evidence must agree. But the Chief Priests were in a hurry to get Jesus tried and sentenced and put to death. Everything had to be finished before Saturday, the sacred sabbath day. Already it was Friday, for the Jewish day began at sunset on the day before. They had to finish with Jesus before sunset.

But the witnesses were useless. Even when they were giving evidence together they did not agree.

Peter denies Jesus

Simon Peter and another disciple of Jesus had followed the armed men. When they came to the house of Caiaphas the other disciple followed them inside, for he was known to the household of the High Priest. Peter was left outside. But the other disciple spoke to the maidservant in charge of the door, and she opened it to let Peter in. She looked hard at Peter.

'You too were with Jesus the Nazarene, as was your friend.'

Peter answered quickly, without thinking – 'I don't know him, so I don't know what you mean,' he said awkwardly, in his embarrassment.

It was just after midnight, and somewhere a cock could be heard crowing.

At first Peter kept hidden in the shadows. But it was a cold night, and the servants had a glowing fire of charcoal. They were standing round it, keeping themselves warm during the long wait. In time, Peter came closer to warm himself. The maidservant who had let him in was there, talking with her friends, chatting about the prisoner Jesus and his followers. Then she noticed Peter.

'This man was with Jesus too,' she said, pointing towards Peter.

'I don't know the man!' Peter burst out quickly, as they all stared at him.

Then one of them said, 'She's quite right. I can tell by your speech that you are a man of Galilee.'

Then Peter swore an oath, bringing a curse on himself if he were not telling the truth: 'I swear I don't know the man you're talking about!'

Again the crowing of a cock could be heard. For it was now about four o'clock in the morning, and almost dawn. Then Peter noticed that Jesus, standing alone before his accusers, was looking down the hall toward him. And suddenly he remembered what Jesus had said:

'Before the cock crows twice you will deny me three times.' He knew, now, what he had done. Horrified and heart-broken he rushed out, threw himself on the ground, and wept bitterly.

Jesus is found guilty

Caiaphas had to do something. No two witnesses agreed with each other, and he had no real evidence against Jesus. Nor would Jesus defend himself – he remained silent. Caiaphas decided to question the prisoner himself, to see if he could get some kind of confession. He stood up and faced Jesus.

'Are you the Christ the Son of God?' he demanded.

Now Jesus spoke. For the third time that week, **openly and deliberately, he claimed to be the promised Savior. Again, too, he used the words of a prophet.**

'I am,' Jesus answered the High Priest. 'And you will see the Son of Man sitting at the right hand of God, and coming with the clouds of heaven.'

'Blasphemy!' cried the High Priest. With both hands he tore open the top of his tunic, a solemn sign of protest. 'What need is there of further witnesses? You heard his blasphemy – what is your verdict?'

'Guilty!' came the answer. 'Guilty of death!'

Then some began to spit on Jesus. Others blindfolded him, struck his face with the palms of their hands and cried, 'Now, you prophet, tell us who slapped you!' Even the servants joined in mocking him.

Jesus had openly claimed to be the Messiah of God. That was blasphemy to those who did not believe in him. The penalty for blaspheming against God was stoning to death. Caiaphas and the Chief Priests had got what they wanted. Now they could get rid of Jesus.

This trial of Jesus had been going on during the night. Many rules of justice had been broken. One rule remained – that a trial must be held, and a verdict given, only in the hours of daylight. Now that it was day Caiaphas called everyone to order. Now it was a formal meeting of the Council. The charge, the verdict, and the punishment were soon confirmed.

Jesus was guilty of blasphemy against God. The penalty was death.

Jesus before Pilate

The Romans allowed the Council to judge and punish **offenses against Jewish laws. But it seems that only the** Roman governor could pass sentence of death. Now the Chief Priests had to persuade Pontius Pilate to confirm their sentence, and to order the death of Jesus. They knew that Pilate would not care about blasphemy against their religion. Romans believed in many gods and one was as good as another to them. Jesus must be accused of treason against Rome – nothing less would do.

Pilate received a message from the High Priest that there was an important prisoner to be tried. He must act quickly, to avoid any chance of a riot. He went from his palace to the Castle of Antonia, the Roman headquarters in Jerusalem. Jesus was brought across the city, and stood before Pilate's judgement-seat in the courtyard. The Chief Priests made their false charges against Jesus — he stirred up the people; he told them not to pay Roman taxes; he claimed to be a king. No charges could be more serious to the Roman governor.

Pilate had already made serious blunders in ruling the Jews. He was hard, and obstinate, and without mercy. But even he could see that Jesus was no wild revolutionary – he would not even defend himself. Pilate strode out to the Chief Priests and the crowd of supporters they had gathered.

'Take him yourselves, and judge him by your own law,' he said briskly.

'It is not lawful for us to put anyone to death,' they answered.

Then, in the tumult, Pilate heard the cry, 'He stirs up the people from Galilee to Jerusalem!'

Pilate saw a way out. As Jesus was a man of Galilee he should be judged by Herod, the ruler of Galilee – and Herod was in Jerusalem. So Pilate ordered that Jesus be taken to Herod to be judged. Herod had been wanting to meet the famous prophet for a long time – and to see him work his wonders. But Jesus remained silent, and Herod sent him back to Pilate for him to decide the case.

At least Herod and Pilate became friends that day, after a long enmity between them.

Jesus sentenced to death

Now Pilate had to decide. He could see no threat to Roman rule in Jesus. But the Chief Priests and their followers did not cease shouting for his death. There was still another way to get out of making a decision. There was a popular rebel in prison awaiting death. He had led a riot in which murder had been committed. His name was Jesus Barabbas. Pilate went out to the crowd.

'I will keep the custom of the feast and release one prisoner!' he cried. 'Which Jesus do you want — Jesus called Barabbas, or Jesus called king of the Jews?'

The Chief Priests quickly got their followers to shout together, 'Barabbas! We want Barabbas!'

Then Pilate signed the order for Jesus to be put to death on the cross.

Crucifixion was a terrible way of putting a man to death. The Romans had copied it from the people of

Carthage. It was the death for rebels, and slaves, and criminals. First the condemned man was scourged with cruel whips. Then he was made to carry the heavy cross-bar to the place of execution. There the upright beam of wood was already placed in a hole in the ground. The criminal's hands were nailed to the cross-bar, and he was tied to his cross with ropes. There he hung, just a little above the ground. It might be days before he died.

Jesus dies on the cross

After Jesus had been scourged the Roman soldiers had cruel fun with him. They pretended that he was a king. They made a crown from a thornbush nearby, and thrust it down on his head. They threw the scarlet cloak of a soldier around him, as his royal robe. They pushed a reed into his hand, as his royal scepter. Then they pretended to kneel before him, shouting, 'Hail! King of the Jews!'

When they had finished their fun with Jesus they took off the cloak, and put his own cloak over him. They led him out, staggering under the heavy beam for his cross. The place of execution was Skull Hill, just outside the city wall. There Jesus was crucified, together with two thieves, one on either side of him. The usual placard was fixed above his cross. It said *Jesus of Nazareth King of the Jews*. It was written three times – in Hebrew, the language of Jews; in Latin, the language of Romans; and in the language of Greeks.

Jesus was crucified at nine o'clock in the morning.

Four soldiers were on guard there. They shared the clothes of a condemned man, so the cloak of Jesus was theirs. It was woven in one piece, without seams, too good to cut into four pieces. They decided to dice for it, to settle which of them should have it.

A group of weeping women, disciples of Jesus, stood by the cross. Among them was Mary, the mother of Jesus. John the apostle was with her, and Jesus committed his mother to John's care. The other apostles were in hiding, save for Judas Iscariot. He had hanged himself, in bitter remorse for what he had done.

About midday it began to get dark. Jesus lingered on, and he was heard saying to himself the words of a psalm. About three o'clock he cried with a loud voice, 'My work is finished!' Then he said the bedtime prayer of every Jewish child: 'Father, into thy hands I commend my spirit.' So he died.

The Chief Priests wanted to make sure that Jesus was dead before sunset, when the sabbath day began. For the sacred law said that a body must not hang on the cross during the sabbath. Pilate gave permission for breaking the legs of the three crucified men, so that they would die quickly. When the soldiers came to Jesus they found him already dead.

That Friday was a terrible day for disciples of Jesus. All their hopes and beliefs had died with Jesus. Yet it was to become Good Friday. For it was on that day that Jesus completed his work of suffering love. Now he was to rise up in glory.

Jesus lives

OSEPH OF ARIMATHAEA was a secret disciple of Jesus and came from a small town in the hills near Jerusalem. He was a rich and devout man, and a member of the Council. He had not agreed when the Council condemned Jesus, but neither had he spoken up for Jesus. He had been filled with sorrow as he watched Jesus die on the cross. But now there was something he could do, to show his devotion to Jesus. He went boldly to Pilate, and got permission to bury the body of Jesus. The burial had to be done quickly, before sunset. For then the sacred sabbath day began and no work of any kind whatever was permitted on the sabbath.

Joseph had a friend to help him. He was Nicodemus, a devout man and a Pharisee. He too was wealthy, and a member of the Council like Joseph. He also had been attracted by Jesus, and had even gone to talk with him. But he went to Jesus in the darkness of night, so that no one could see him. Now he could help his friend Joseph to show his own devotion to Jesus.

Joseph owned a garden in Jerusalem, and it lay just beside Skull Hill, where Jesus had been crucified. In his garden he had had a tomb cut out of the rock. It was for himself and his family, so that they might rest for ever at the holy city, when death came to them. Now his tomb could be used, for the first time, to honor Jesus. There was no time to arrange for mourners, or to embalm the body, according to custom. Joseph and Nicodemus wrapped the body of Jesus in white linen burial sheets, with scented spices of myrrh and aloes. They wrapped a separate cloth around his head. Then they laid him in Joseph's new tomb, watched by Mary of Magdala and another woman disciple of Jesus.

Tombs were easily cut in the soft limestone rock. Mourners had to stoop down to pass through the low entrance to the tomb. It had two chambers. The first was a tiny room, with a ledge all round it, where mourners could sit to share their grief. Then another low entrance led into the burial chamber, where the body was laid on a ledge cut in the wall. A family tomb would have several ledges cut like this for its members.

Tombs were guarded. For things of value were often buried with the dead, and tombs of rich and noble persons were robbed for their treasures. The best kind of guard was a big, heavy, rounded stone, shaped like a solid wheel. A grove for it was cut in the rock, outside the entrance to the tomb. The stone rolled down the groove, and covered the entrance. So the only way of getting into the tomb was by rolling the heavy stone upwards, and then fixing it with a wedge, to stop it from rolling down again. It would take several strong men to open a tomb guarded by a stone like this.

Mary of Magdala at the tomb

Mary of Magdala and the other woman disciple had watched the burial of Jesus, so they knew where the tomb was. They had to leave it, soon after Joseph and Nicodemus, for dusk was coming on and the sabbath about to begin. Nothing could be done till the sabbath ended at dusk on the following day. So it was on the first day of the week, our Sunday, that the women could perform their last act of love for Jesus – to embalm his body, according to custom, with the burial spices. It was still dark when they set out for the tomb. They would wait there for gardeners or passers-by to roll back the stone so that they could enter the tomb.

But a shock awaited them when they reached the tomb – the stone had been rolled away already. They hurried back to tell the apostles. Peter and John ran to the tomb. John got there first, but it was Peter who stooped down and went right inside to the burial chamber. It was empty. The linen cloths lay on the ledge. The burial cloth, which had been wound around the head of Jesus, lay separate, still rolled up like an empty ball. The body of Jesus had gone.

The apostles did not know what to think as they walked slowly back. Mary of Magdala stayed behind in the garden, weeping bitterly. Through her tears she saw someone standing there, and took him for the gardener when he spoke to her.

'Why are you weeping? Who are you looking for?'

'Oh, sir,' she wept, 'if you have taken him away please tell me where he is, so that I may give him burial.'

'Mary,' he said softly. It was the voice she knew so well. Startled and astonished she looked up. It was Jesus standing before her.

'Master!' she cried out in her joy, and threw herself at his feet.

'Don't stay here, clinging to me,' Jesus said gently. 'Go and tell my disciples.'

'I have seen the Lord!' Mary cried when she got back to the upper room and eagerly began her wonderful story.

The walk of Emmaus

That same afternoon, two disciples of Jesus were walking to the village of Emmaus, several miles from Jerusalem. They were Cleopas and his friend, who had both been followers of Jesus. They were going back to their home village, full of sorrow. It was all over now. Jesus was dead, and that was the end. How tragic it seemed to them, that his wonderful life and work should come to nothing.

A stranger joined them on the road. 'Why are you so sad?' he asked them. They were astonished.

'You must be the only stranger in Jerusalem who hasn't heard the dreadful things that have happened,' they said to him.

'What things?' the stranger asked.

Then they told him of Jesus, the prophet and teacher, whom they had believed to be the Messiah of God. But how could he be, if he died so tragically, they said. They told the stranger, too, how that very morning the women had found his tomb empty, and could not find him anywhere.

'What foolish men you are,' said the stranger, 'so slow to believe what the prophets have written. They told how the Messiah must suffer, and die, and then enter into his glory.'

The stranger went on to explain the sacred writings which had told of the coming Savior. Cleopas and has

124

friend listened eagerly as the stranger gave them new hope. In no time they reached Emmaus, and the stranger made as if to walk on.

'Come in and have supper with us,' the two friends pleaded. 'It is nearly dark, and you can't go on through the night.'

So the stranger went in, and sat at the table with them. And, while they were eating, he took a flat round loaf of bread, blessed it, broke it, and gave it to them. Then their eyes were opened and they recognised the stranger – Jesus. And he vanished from their sight.

'No wonder that our hearts burned as he talked to us!' they cried. They hurried back to Jerusalem to tell the disciples how Jesus was made known to them in the breaking of bread.

In the upper room

Cleopas and his friend had hardly finished telling their story to the apostles when Jesus appeared to them. They met together in the upper room secretly, with the door bolted, fearing that the Chief Priests might persecute the followers of Jesus. They were terrified when Jesus suddenly appeared, as if he were a ghost.

'Why are you troubled, and full of doubt?' said Jesus. 'See my hands and my feet, that it is really I myself. A ghost does not have flesh and bones as I have.'

Then Jesus spoke to them, explaining how all the hopes of the prophets had been fulfilled in him. Now the kingdom of God must be preached among men, and they were to be his witnesses.

Thomas, one of the apostles, was not with them that evening. When he returned they told him how Jesus had appeared to them. But Thomas was full of doubt. 'I won't believe it unless I see him, and touch him for myself,' he said.

A week later Thomas was with them in the upper room, with the door barred. Jesus appeared and stood before them.

'Peace be unto you,' he said to them. Then he turned to Thomas, stretching out his hands. 'See my hands, touch me, and believe,' Jesus said.

'My Lord and my God!' Thomas cried, as he fell on his knees.

'Do you believe because you have seen me?' said Jesus. 'How blessed are those who have not seen me, and yet believe in me.'

By the seashore

Some nights later, Simon Peter and the other fishermen apostles had gone out in their boat. They had let down their nets a little way offshore. Morning came, and they had caught nothing. In the early mist they could see

someone on the shore. He called out to them to cast
their nets on the other side of the boat. They tried this,
and their nets were soon full. Then John said to Peter,
'It is the Lord!'

Peter grabbed his cloak and scrambled ashore, the
others following in the boat, with the heavy catch.

After they had eaten breakfast, Jesus said to Peter,
'Simon, do you love me?'

'Yes, Lord, you know that I love you.'

'Feed my sheep,' said Jesus.

Jesus asked him a second time, and again Peter swore
his love. But when Jesus asked him a third time he was
deeply grieved. He had been a broken man ever since
that night he denied Jesus. He felt that he had failed
Jesus. He was useless. Now he had lost all faith in
himself. But he was sure of one thing – he loved Jesus
with all his heart.

'Lord, you know everything!' he cried. 'You know
that I love you!'

'Be a shepherd to my flock,' Jesus said to him.

Then Peter knew that Jesus needed him – he was not
useless. Jesus trusted him and he could have faith in
himself. Now Jesus was calling him to new service as a
fisher of men, a shepherd of his sheep, a laborer
gathering in the harvest of God's kingdom.

Now Peter was a new man, filled with new faith and
courage to serve his Master to the end.

Jesus lives

The time came for Jesus to leave his disciples. He led
them up the hill of Bethany, and there gave them his
parting message: 'You will receive power when the Spirit
of God comes upon you. You will be my witnesses,
spreading the Good News to the ends of the earth.'

Then, suddenly, the cloud of the glory of God shone round about Jesus. And when it was gone they saw him no more.

The apostles returned to Jerusalem full of joy. They joined in the daily services of the Temple, singing the praises of God. They met together in the upper room, where they had shared that Last Supper with their Lord. There they remembered the Lord Jesus in the breaking of bread, and in their prayers, and knew that he was present with them.

It was there, ten days later on the Feast of Pentecost, that the power which Jesus had promised came upon them. Suddenly the morning sun seemed like fire, setting their hearts ablaze. The morning breeze seemed like a hurricane, blowing new life into them. And they were filled with the Holy Spirit of God. They rushed down from the upper room full of power, and began shouting aloud the Good News of Jesus. A crowd quickly gathered and Peter spoke to them of Jesus. He called them to change their minds and hearts, and to be **baptized in the name of Jesus the Christ, so as to receive** forgiveness of sins and the gift of the Holy Spirit. That very day, hundreds believed the Good News and were baptised. It was the birthday of the Christian Church, the family of believers in Jesus the Christ.

The Church of Jesus began with those few disciples in Jerusalem. Today, 2,000 years later, there are Christian churches all over the world. Why is it that the Church of Jesus lives on, while earthly empires rise and fall? It is because Christians believe in a living Lord. They know his presence among them. They feel his **power within them.** They have his Good News to guide them in all their ways. They know that Jesus lives.

Houses

The houses which Jesus and his friends knew were mainly very simple, square, one-roomed buildings, with flat roofs, and just a single storey. They were built from baked mud, bricks, stone and wood. Some were poorly built, and might be washed away by a heavy rainstorm. The best houses were usually made of stone. As the family became larger, or more wealthy, it was easy to add on another apartment. There are still many houses around the Mediterranean Sea like this today. There were very few isolated buildings; at this time many robbers and brigands (like the ones who attacked the man in the parable of the Good Samaritan) roamed the countryside, and it was far safer to live near other people.

Simple Houses

Most houses had just one floor, which was split into two levels, instead of being divided by a wall. The upper level was a platform for sleeping, and for keeping cooking utensils, while the lower level was used for keeping animals at night. An outside staircase led up to the flat roof which was surrounded by a parapet. In hot weather, people would often sleep on the roof, under a canopy. The roof could also be used for drying or ripening vegetables and fruit, and for praying. Roofs were usually of very light materials, often branches covered with mud, resting on the solid beams. It would have been quite possible to make a hole in the roof, and let someone into a house from above, as the sick man's friend did at Capernaum.

128

Life in the time of Jesus

Inside

There was very little furniture inside these houses. People used rugs or mats for beds, which they laid out on the raised half of the floor. They usually slept in their day clothes, and so there were no sheets or blankets. It would have been very easy to carry your bed around with you. Richer people sometimes had mattresses, which were stuffed with straw or feathers. A whole family slept together side by side on the platform, like Levi's friend Simeon, who did not want to get out of bed and disturb his children (Luke 11.5-13).

Cooking utensils and pots were kept in little niches cut into the mud walls of the house. The house was lit by oil lamps at night and wealthy people would have many different lampstands and brackets. There would have been a few low tables, perhaps a couch, and a brazier.

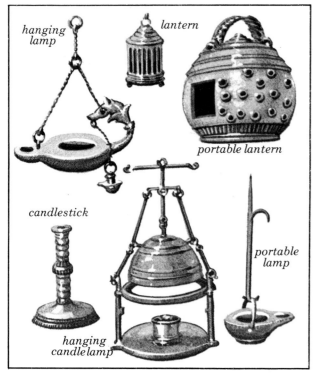

hanging lamp

lantern

portable lantern

candlestick

portable lamp

hanging candle lamp

Heating

Many houses had a hollow in the middle of the floor, which was filled with wood or charcoal. When the embers died down, boards and rugs were pulled across it, so that the floor retained the heat. Other people used the heat from the brazier, after they had done their cooking, for warmth. They stood round it to keep warm, as the people in Caiaphas' house were doing when Jesus was arrested (Mark 14.54).

The publisher acknowledges with thanks permission to use as reference two illustrations by Majorie Quennell from *Everyday Life in New Testament Times*, published by B.T. Batsford Ltd.

Inns

In the time of Jesus, inns were not like our hotels. They were often dirty places, and had bad reputations because of the criminal and immoral dealings that often went on within their walls. They were usually by the sides of the main roads, and provided stables for weary animals. Wealthy travellers could pay for a private room in the main building, but most people had to sleep in a covered area near the courtyard, where the animals were housed. Travellers usually provided their own food and drink, and brought their beds with them.

Large Houses

The larger houses were built around a central courtyard, and had very few windows. This helped to keep the house cool, and the courtyard provided shade, where perhaps there might be a few trees. All the rooms opened inwards, or into other rooms, rather than out on to the narrow streets. There was no police force, so it was much safer to build a house in this way. The richer families would employ a porter to look after the main entrance.

Some of these houses had two floors, and the best rooms, for visitors, would be on the higher floors. The storerooms and treasure chests would be in secret rooms opening off the inner apartments.

Occupations

The towns and villages which Jesus visited were filled with the sounds of people going about their various trades – skilled craftsmen like carpenters, potters, weavers and stonemasons. Many people worked on the land, as farmers, sowing and gathering their crops, or tending their trees and vines. People who lived by the Sea of Galilee were mostly fishermen. In the towns there were tax collectors and bankers, innkeepers, musicians, and the scribes and rabbis of the synagogues.

Farming

The land of Jesus was a very rich and fertile land. The most important crops were wheat, barley, olives, dates, figs, grapes and pomegranates.

The farmer used very simple tools to do his work, and methods have altered little in Palestine since then. He would sow his crops – usually wheat or barley, after the rains in autumn. Like the sower in Jesus' story, he would carry a basket from which he would scatter the seeds. Most farmers nowadays plough before they sow, but in Jesus' time the farmers would plough the land afterward, to cover up the seeds. They used simple wooden ploughs tipped with iron plough shares and drawn by oxen. Another method was just to let cattle trample over the land, pushing the seeds into the earth. Until harvest time the farmer was kept busy harrowing the fields.

Harvesting

The spring harvest was usually ripe by April or May, and the whole family would be in the fields reaping the corn with sickles, and building corn sheaves which could be carried to the threshing floor. If the farmer could afford it, he would often hire extra workers to help with this.

The threshing area was a circle of hard ground, surrounded by a wall, usually in a place where the wind could carry away the chaff. The corn was trampled by oxen, and then winnowed, which means turning it with a fork and tossing it into the air with rakes. The grain would fall to the ground and the husks would blow away. The grain would then be sieved and stored in granaries (Matthew 13.30). Often the farmer had someone to guard these for he had to make sure that thieves did not steal his crop.

Life in the time of Jesus

Fruit Growing

There were many vineyards, and these were well cared for. The vines were allowed to grow along the ground, or over trellises, and when the fruit began to form the bunches of grapes would be supported with poles.

Most vineyards had a little watchman's hut, built out of the stones which lay scattered around the vineyard. This was because foxes and jackals were attracted to the fruit, and often raided the vines, so someone had to be permanently on guard.

Harvest times were always the scenes of much festivity, and families camped out in the vineyards while the grapes were gathered. Most of the fruit was pressed to make wine, but a small amount would be left to dry in the sun to make raisins.

The olive was one of the most important fruits, since it provided much oil. One tree could give up to 17 gallons. The trees grew in orchards, but as many trees had different owners, everyone had to wait until the priest declared the date for the harvest. The trees were beaten and shaken, but the laws said that you could only do this once. Afterward, the poor people were allowed to glean what had been left.

Olives were pressed in wooden presses, which were turned by hand, or by a donkey harnessed to the handle, to extract all the oil. Some were put aside and preserved. The Garden of Gethsemane was an olive grove, since the word Gethsemane means 'olive press'.

Other farmers owned fig trees or date palms, or pomegranate trees. A few vegetables and pulse crops like beans and lentils were grown, and some people also had small herb gardens.

Shepherds

Shepherds worked very differently in Palestine in the time of Jesus. Instead of driving their sheep with dogs, as they do now, they would lead them, by calling or by playing a flute.

Young shepherds like Benjamin had to learn to call their sheep, and also to protect them. Each shepherd carried a club and a sling to ward off wild animals. At that time, wolves, foxes and jackals were a constant danger, and there were even bears in the hills. In Old Testament times many lions and cheetahs roamed around, and although there were very few left by the time of Jesus, they were still feared by the shepherds (John 10.11-13).

The sheep kept were mainly the fat-tailed variety. Their tails could weigh up to 13 pounds, and they stored fat in the same way as a camel's hump does. Goats were also kept, mixed in with the flocks. Every evening the shepherd led his sheep to water, and then they were counted as they were driven into a pen for the night. The shepherd slept across the entrance to the pen, protecting his flocks.

Sheep were very valuable as they not only provided meat and milk, but also fleece and leather, and the young lambs were still offered as sacrifices. It was very important to make sure that none were lost.

131

Craftsmen

Not all craftsmen worked in their own homes; there is evidence of some small factories, and in large towns whole streets would often be taken over by one trade and named after that trade. Sizes of goods such as pots were sometimes standardized.

Stewards

Most slaves lived as part of the family, and were given their board, and a place to sleep. Often they were given positions of trust, as stewards. When their master was away they had to look after his land and property. Good stewards might be rewarded with freedom.

Fishermen

Most of the people who lived on the shores of the Lake of Galilee had jobs that were in some way connected with fishing. Most of the fishing in Palestine went on here, as there were no fish in the Dead Sea, and few people fished in the Mediterranean at this time.

Fishermen often grouped together in teams of six or more so that they could afford to buy a boat and nets between them. They would share out the profits from the catch afterwards.

There were several methods of fishing. Some nets were round, and weighted round the edges. These were dropped over the top of the shoals and hauled back into the boats when they were full. Other nets had weights along one edge and floats on the other. The boat was rowed out, with one end of the net, whilst someone held the other end on the shore. The net was then lowered into the water and the man in the boat rowed back in a semicircle, so that all the fish in that area were enclosed by the net. The net was then hauled in.

Once on land, the fish had to be very carefully sorted.

Some fresh fish was sent to the local markets, but the rest had to be salted and pickled or dried, as there was usually too much to eat all at once.

Carpenters

The carpenter had to be very adaptable, as he was expected to do a great many things. A carpenter like Joseph had to be able to make furniture, doors, cart wheels and tools for the farmer and for other craftsmen. He might also be asked to build a boat for the fishermen, and he had to be artistic, so that his work would look attractive. Some wood was used in building houses, so the carpenter often worked closely with the stonemason.

Stonemasons

The stonemason had to be very skilful as very little mortar was used in building and the stones had to be laid very carefully. The stone had to be quarried, and then shaped by the mason. Tombs, and storage cellars, were often cut out of the soft limestone rock.

Life in the time of Jesus

Dyers

Dyeing was quite common in Palestine at this time. Many vegetable dyes were used, and the cochineal insect was known, and used for red cloths for the synagogues. Purple dye, which was very expensive, was obtained from shell-fish, and only used for special garments. Only rulers and wealthy men wore costly purple robes.

Tanners and Fullers

The work of these people was considered unclean, as it involved handling the hides of dead animals, some of which, like the camel, were 'unclean'. Tanners and fullers therefore had to work outside the towns, near streams. The fuller had the job of scouring and bleaching sheeps' fleeces, which was very unpleasant, and the tanner had to treat the hides ready for the leather workers.

Slaves

Some men, like shepherds and farmers, worked for themselves as free men. So too did workers in crafts and trades. All these workers hired **laborers to work under them. Another group** of workers was slaves. They belonged to the household and worked in the house and on the family land. But slaves were higher than hired **laborers. These common laborers had noth-**ing except what odd jobs they could get. This was all that the lost son could hope for when he went back home (Luke 15.18-19). Slaves were part of the household. They had a home and food and work. They were protected by the sacred law of the Jews. They could be rewarded for loyal service, and even be given their freedom. It was better to belong to a household than to be a beggar on the streets.

Tax Collectors

Tax collectors and money lenders were very unpopular, because many of them were very corrupt. In addition to their own Temple tax the Jews had to pay various taxes to the Romans, which they bitterly hated. Wealthy merchants often bribed tax-collectors to let them off their taxes. A Jew paid the Romans for the right to collect their hated taxes. He squeezed all he could from his people so as to make a good profit for himself. They despised him for being a traitor and for making money out of them.

Unemployment

Not everyone was lucky enough to have a job, and those who were seeking work used to gather in the market places in the morning. People who needed workmen would come here and bargain with them for their pay. Some men would group together in teams, and at harvest times they would travel from farm to farm, offering their services. There was a great need for regular work and wages, for families would receive no support from the state, as they do now. It was not surprising that many people did choose to become slaves, for the sake of a secure income.

Roman Rule

When the Romans conquered a country they brought justice and law, order and peace, new buildings and fine roads, and trade with other lands. Palestine became part of the Roman Empire in 63 B.C. Herod the Great was made king of the Jews. He kept law and order by ruling as a tyrant. His eldest son became king of Judaea after him. But he was foolish and weak and the Romans had to dismiss him. A Roman Governor, called a Procurator, was appointed in his place. Pontius Pilate was the Procurator from 26 to 36 A.D. The Jews hated Pilate and his men. They had conquered the Jews. They were Gentiles and pagans, lording it over God's people. The Jews never submitted to them.

Roman Taxation

A conquered people had to pay for Roman rule. There were taxes on everyone, taxes on property, on food, on land, death duties and purchase tax. The Romans sold the right to collect taxes to the highest bidders every five years. These tax collectors made sure of getting their money back and of making a good profit too. So they made people pay more than the exact tax that was due. It was worse for Jews because they had their own taxes to pay — the Temple tax and their religious dues. No wonder they hated Jews who collected Roman taxes.

Roman Army

Military service was another way a conquered people paid for Roman rule. The Romans raised troops called auxiliaries in conquered lands to help the famous legions. They did garrison duty and kept order while the legions were reserved for active service. They guarded prisoners too, as at the trial and crucifixion of Jesus (Mark 15.16-24).

Jews were exempt from doing this military service. For their religion did not permit them to carry arms on the sabbath, and the Romans did not want soldiers who would serve on only six days of the week.

Conquered people also had to pay reverence to the Roman Emperor as a god. The Romans had to exempt the Jews from this too. They soon learned that Jews would rather die than worship any other god. They learned too how offended Jews were by their religious military ceremonies.

tribune   legionary   centurion   auxiliary

Roman Census

Every 14 years the Romans ordered a census to be taken. This counting of the people was so that they could be taxed. Everyone knew this and a census often caused a revolt. The rule was that anyone who had moved away from his home town had to return there for the census. That was why Joseph had to return to Bethlehem, taking Mary with him, for it was his family home (Luke 2.1-5).

Roman Citizenship

It was a great privilege to be born a free citizen of the Roman empire, as Paul was. Auxiliary troops serving in the Roman army were given this privilege. Men paid large sums of money for this honor too (Acts 22.27-28). Everyone got fair justice in a court of law. But a Roman citizen charged in a law-court could always demand to be tried before the emperor himself. Paul claimed this right when he saw that there was no hope of getting justice in Jerusalem and he was taken by ship to Rome itself.

Life in the time of Jesus
Transport

The people of Jesus had no love of travel. Jews never went far by land, except as pilgrims, and they were terrified of the sea. Most Jews never went far from home, so their roads were no more than rough tracks between towns and villages. The journey for pilgrims from Nazareth in the north to Jerusalem in the south was 72 miles and it took three days. For journeys had to be made on foot, with only donkeys to carry the loads. All forms of travel at that time were hazardous. There was the danger of being attacked by wild animals or of being set upon by robbers.

Romans

It was quite different for Romans. Their famous roads were the key to rapid communication, and the Roman empire was kept together by their roads. Their couriers, carrying despatches on fast horses, covered 45 miles or more in a day. Their legions of disciplined soldiers could be moved swiftly to wherever there was trouble. Roman roads were solidly built and many are still used today. They were built in three layers. The bottom layer was made of stones mixed with cement; above that was a mixture of rubble, gravel, rough stone or broken pottery; the top layer was made of large stones fitting tightly together. These roads linked each of the provinces with Rome. They made possible the Roman system of trade, government, law and order which gave the famous Roman 'pax' or 'peace'.

Jews

In Palestine the main Roman roads were along the coast and east of the river Jordan, running between north and south, with a road across the plain of Esdraelon between them. All other roads were rough and pitted with holes. Ordinary folk had only donkeys or mules for riding. Only Romans had horses, used mainly by couriers and troops. Romans also had wheeled carriages and wagons drawn by horses and mules. Common folk had carts to carry heavy loads. But in hilly regions they depended on sure-footed donkeys and mules which could carry heavy burdens.

A great deal of long-distance travel within the Roman empire was by sea. Sailing ships could carry six hundred people or more for travel or for cruises. Regular ships sailed from North Africa to Rome with corn for feeding the great city. In winter only vital sea journeys were made for the waters of the Mediterranean Sea were too dangerous in rough wintery weather. Only lightly built warships had oars, so that all through the year ships were dependent on favorable winds for a fast journey.

135

Religion

The Jews, the people of Jesus, believed in the one God who had called them to be his Chosen People. In the beginning he had called Abraham, the founder of the Jewish people. Later he had called Moses to give the Jews his sacred laws. They were written in the Bible of the Jews, and the people of Jesus lived by them. Still today Jews live by the sacred laws and traditions and ways of worship which Jesus knew. In the land of Jesus there were Greeks and Romans who believed in many Gods. They were quite different from Jews in their way of life.

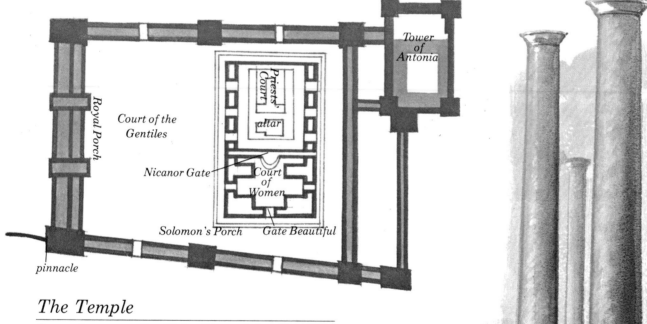

Tower of Antonia

Royal Porch

Priests' Court

altar

Court of the Gentiles

Nicanor Gate

Court of Women

Solomon's Porch

Gate Beautiful

pinnacle

The Temple

Jerusalem was the Holy City of the Jews, for there was the Temple of God. Herod the Great, the ruler appointed by the Romans, rebuilt the Temple. He hoped that would make him more popular with the Jews who regarded him as a foreigner. Herod had a thousand priests trained to do the building, so that the Temple area would be kept sacred in the eyes of Jews. Herod's Temple was built in dazzling white marble, decorated with gold, and with golden spires on the roof to prevent birds nesting there. The main building took ten years and this was the Temple that Jesus knew (eg. Mark 13.1). It was still not finished when it was destroyed in 70 A.D.

Life in the time of Jesus

The Temple Tax

When Jews reached the age of twenty years they had to pay a tax for the upkeep of the Temple. It had to be paid each year at the Passover Festival in special money. Jews used the money of other lands, for minting their own coins might break the sacred commandment against making 'graven images'. Jews who came to Jerusalem from other lands brought even more foreign coins. Money-changers in the courtyard of the Temple changed foreign coins into the special money needed for paying the tax. It had always been a silver coin called a half-shekel. But in the time of Jesus it could be paid in Greek silver coins called drachmas. The tax was two drachmas, and it was paid with the didrachma (two drachmas) *(left)* or the tetra-drachma (four drachmas) shown *right*.

Passover

The Passover has always been the greatest Festival of the year for Jews. In early times it was a spring festival when shepherds gave thanks for the newborn lambs. From the time of Moses it commemorated for ever how God had delivered his Chosen People from slavery in Egypt. Its name came from the time when the angel of death "passed over" the homes of the Jewish slaves (Exodus 12. 12-14). It was the **duty of all Jewish males living within 15 miles of Jerusalem to go to the Temple for** the Passover, just as Jesus did (Luke 2.41-42; 22.1-8). But Jews who lived in other lands came from all over the world for the Passover. The pilgrims travelled in large groups, or caravans, to avoid attacks by robbers. Each family, or group of friends, bought a young lamb which they offered as a sacrifice in the Temple. Then it was taken home and roasted for the sacred meal. The meal also included unleavened bread, a symbol of the hasty flight from Egypt; bitter herbs and parsley, symbols of the bitter life of slaves in Egypt; and four cups of wine, drunk with special psalms and prayers. During the solemn meal the eldest son asked the meaning of the Feast. Then the story of the wonderful deliverance from Egypt was told again, so that it would never be forgotten.

Festivals

The second great Festival of the year was called Pentecost, which means 'fiftieth', for it came fifty days after Passover. It was the Harvest Festival of the new corn, when loaves of bread were offered in the Temple. It had become the Festival of the giving of the Law to Moses, when Jews praised God for the sacred laws by which they lived.

The third great Festival of the year, in the autumn, was the Harvest of grapes and olives and fruits. It had become a memorial of the years of wandering in the wilderness when the Jews of old lived in tents or tabernacles. During this Feast of Tabernacles Jews lived in tents made with branches as a symbol of their forefathers.

Another popular Festival each year was the Feast of Lights. It celebrated the time when the Jews had won back the Temple from the Greek ruler who tried to destroy their religion. The Temple had been restored to the worship of God and its sacred lamps relit. So during this Feast the Jews lit lamps and torches and candles in their homes and synagogues and in the Temple. It may have been at this festival that Jesus said: "I am the light of the world" (John 8.12; 10.22-3).

Each year there were fasts as well as feasts. Fasts were times when Jews went without food and drink to show sorrow to God for their wrong-doing. The most solemn fast of the year began with the New Year Festival called Rosh Hashanah, marked by the blowing of a ram's horn. Then followed ten days of penitence, ending with the solemn Yom Kippur or Day of Atonement when sacrifice was made in the Temple to cleanse the people of their sins against God.

Seven-branched Candlestick

Seven was a sacred number to the Jews, and there had always been seven-branched candlesticks in the Temple. The most sacred part of the Temple was the Holy of Holies, pitch dark and empty save for the seven-branched candlestick which was the symbol of the presence of God. Still today it is the symbol of God in Jewish synagogues and it can be seen in Jewish synagogues throughout the world.

Synagogue

Sacrifices could only be offered in the Temple at Jerusalem. So another kind of worship grew up when Jews were taken away as captives to other lands. By the time of Jesus most Jews lived in other lands. They worshipped God in synagogues which means 'meeting-places'. Any ten Jews could set up a synagogue, so there were thousands of synagogues in towns all over the Roman world. On the sabbath, and on other special days, Jews met in their synagogues to worship God. They held public meetings there too, for the synagogue was the center of their life. By day it was used as a school where Jewish boys studied the sacred writings of their Bible. That was why the synagogue had two names – House of Prayer and House of Study.

There could be no sacrifice in the synagogue, so there was no altar. The most sacred place was the 'ark' where the scrolls of the sacred writings were kept, with a lamp always burning above it. During the service there were readings from the sacred writings, an address, hymns and prayers. Any Jew might be invited to read a lesson and to give an address – just as Jesus was in the synagogue at Nazareth where he had been to school (Luke 4.16-22).

Life in the time of Jesus

Mazuzah

At the door of every Jewish house was a small case of wood or metal, fixed to the righthand door-post, called the Mazuzah. Inside it was a small piece of skin on which was written a text telling the Jewish belief in one God (Deuteronomy 6.4-5). It was called the Shema from its first word, which means 'Hear'. Anyone entering or leaving the house touched the Mazuzah. Then he kissed the hand which had touched the sacred text-box and said the prayer: "May God keep my going out and my coming in" (Psalm 121.8).

Phylacteries

Jewish men and boys over the age of twelve years wore phylacteries or 'guards' for saying their morning prayers. They were little pouches made of skin. Inside each phylactery were four passages from the sacred laws, written on tiny pieces of parchment bound with hair, and 'guarded' by the pouch. One was worn on the forehead, fastened by a leather strap which was wound round the head. The other was worn on the left arm so that when the arm was bent the sacred texts lay over the heart. Its strap, wound seven times round the forearm, was tied with a knot to form the first letter of a Jewish name for God. So the two phylacteries were symbols of dedicating head and heart and hand to the service of God.

Sabbath

The Jewish word 'shabbath' means 'to cease'. In early times the sabbath was the weekly day of rest when men and animals 'ceased' from their daily labors. It became a day sacred to God, and laws grew up to make sure that it was strictly kept. For on the seventh day God had rested from all his work of creation. The sabbath began at sunset on Friday and ended at sunset on Saturday. No work or travelling could be done on the sabbath, not even getting food, or lighting fires, or cooking. Jews wore their best clothes and, after joining in the worship of God at the synagogue, spent the day at home with good food and rest. Jesus went regularly to the synagogue on the sabbath (Luke 4.16). But he spoke against customs and rules which made the sabbath day a burden – and even prevented men from doing good on God's own day (Mark 3.1-5). Even doctors were forbidden to work, except to assist at a birth, on the Sabbath.

Dress

In New Testament times it was often possible to tell a person's standing simply by the clothes he wore. Rich people used expensive fabrics, Roman soldiers wore uniform and Roman officials often wore the toga. Ordinary Jews who worked in the fields or were fishermen could usually be recognized by their tunics, which were tucked into their belts to allow them more movement.

Men

Jewish men wore three garments. Underneath was a long linen garment, a kind of shirt. Then came the main garment, a loose flowing tunic with large sleeves, woven from wool in bright colors. There were no buttons or pins so the tunic was gathered in at the waist with a piece of cloth. The folds of this cloth belt were used as pockets. A man often tucked his tunic up into his belt to leave his legs free. Workers like fishermen 'girded up their loins' as this was called.

The third garment was a thick cloak, like an overcoat, which kept out the heat of day and the cold of night, and could be used as a blanket or a bed. It was made of wool or goat's hair or camel hair. Devout Jews had four blue tassels hanging from the corners of their cloaks. These were religious symbols marking a Jew off from people of other races. We know that Jesus wore these tassels for a woman took hold of one believing that this would bring her the healing powers of Jesus (Mark 5.25-34).

Women

The Bible uses the same words for the garments of both men and women. Women's clothes were similar to men's, but they were made of finer cloth and brighter colors and were embroidered. They certainly looked very different from men's clothes, for the sacred law strictly forbade either sex to wear clothes of the other. Women also wore ribbons, shawls, and rings on both fingers and toes. But men as well as women wore jewellery.

140

Life in the time of Jesus

Head

Out of doors heads had to be covered from the fierce heat of the sun. A simple scarf tied round the head would do for protection. Later a square cloth was used, folded into a triangle, and kept in place by a ring of wool or goat's hair woven like a rope. Married women always covered their hair out of doors, wearing long veils. At special times they held it in place with a chain of coins which had been the woman's dowry (Luke 15.8-9).

Feet

Shoes or sandals were worn on the feet, without socks or stockings. Shoes were made from animal skin, with soles made from rushes or the bark of palm trees. Shoes were soft, but sandals were made of hard leather and even hobnailed for long journeys. A sandal was simply a sole tied to the foot by a thong or latchet which went over the top of the foot and round the ankle (Mark 1.7). At home poor folk went barefoot, and so did servants in a rich man's house. Travellers went barefoot when it was suitable to do so, and saved their sandal leather for the town. Going barefoot was also a sign of mourning.

Making Clothes

Linen was made from flax growing in Galilee and wool came from the sheep of Judaea. A housewife combed, spun and wove her wool on her own loom to make family clothes. Rich people paid the weavers and dyers and fullers to do it for them. In a poor home clothes were handed down from older to younger children and the housewife was often patching (Matthew 9.16).

Best Clothes

Best clothes were kept in a chest in the house, and of course moths were a nuisance (Matthew 6.19-21). These clothes were only worn for special occasions like weddings. For a man to wear his ordinary clothes to a wedding would be an insult (Matthew 22.11-14). A man without party clothes could borrow from a friend or neighbor, for borrowing clothes was quite common. But even the poorest peasants washed and cleaned their working clothes for a special occasion.

Rich Men's Clothes

Only rulers and rich men were 'clothed in fine purple' — that is, in robes dyed with the precious rich red-blue colour known as 'royal purple' which came from Phoenicia. Jewish rabbis regarded purple as pagan, as well as extravagant. But wealthy Jews loved to dress in lawn tunics and purple robes (Luke 16.19). Well-to-do merchants and government officials could afford the fine silk imported from the East. Some wore a fine turban with fringes, closely wound round their heads.

Roman Clothes

Roman soldiers wore a woollen shirt with short sleeves, a woollen cloak reaching to the knees and fastened on the shoulder with a clasp, and a belt. Officers wore long red cloaks.

The toga was the mark of a Roman citizen and foreigners were forbidden to wear it. It was a wide piece of cloth, cut in a semi-circle, and fastened round the body with the straight side uppermost. Pontius Pilate must have worn the toga edged with a purple stripe that was a special honor.

People I

Many different groups of people are mentioned in the New Testament. Even among the Jews there were many different groups – some of them priests, some of them laymen. Jesus often spoke of these groups of people in his parables, telling us of a hypocritical Pharisee, and a good Samaritan. These stories puzzled people because they upset their ideas of whose behavior was to be praised and whose condemned.

Sadducees

Sadducees were the richest and most powerful group of Jews. They were the priestly families of Jerusalem who ruled over the Temple. They lived on the tithes and the yearly Temple tax which had to be paid by all Jews as their religious duty. They also profited by the trading which they permitted in the Temple courts. Sadducees believed strictly in the old Law of Moses and did not accept changes in religion. Their leader was the High Priest, chosen from the priestly families. He was recognized by the Romans as the leader of the Jewish people. He was chairman of the Council of the Jews, called the Sanhedrin, which was the highest court of law of the Jews in Judaea. The rich and powerful Sadducees were lordly in their ways and unpopular with the people. They were friendly to the Romans, for their wealth and power depended on keeping in with their rulers.

Levites

Levites were servants of priests in the worship of the Temple. They, too, were dedicated by birth to the service of God as descendants of the tribe of Levi. The book of Leviticus in the Bible tells of the religious customs and rights and duties of these holy men.

Only priests could go near the altar and the sacred vessels. Levites were doorkeepers and servants in the Temple services, and it seems that they were responsible for the music at the Temple.

Life in the time of Jesus

Pharisees

Pharisees were devout laymen, not priests or holy men. Their name means 'Separate ones', for they kept strictly apart from pagan people like Romans and Greeks. Like the Sadducees they lived strictly by the old written Law of Moses. But they also lived by unwritten laws and customs which had grown up since. They believed in angels, and in spirits, and in life after death. They lived by their laws in every detail — for example, in giving to God a tithe or tenth of everything they had (Luke 18.10-12). **People honored them for their devotion to God,** and they helped to keep Jewish religion alive. Many of them were good and godly men, but Jesus saw through the insincerity of others (Matthew 23.25-28).

Essenes

The Essenes were the monks of Jewish religion. They lived together in the lonely wilderness near the Dead Sea, growing vegetables for food. They did not own anything but shared their earnings. They did not marry and grew by adopting boys. Their simple white linen garment was a symbol of the purity they sought by their daily worship of God and study of the sacred writings. The monks came from different groups such as Sadducees, and it is possible that John the Baptist, who lived in the wilderness, may have belonged to a group of these monks.

Samaritans

These people lived in Samaria, the land between Judaea in the south and Galilee in the north. Jews travelling between north and south would go across the river Jordan to avoid the Samaritans (John 4.9). They came from Jews who had married foreigners, and there had been a quarrel between pure Jews and Samaritans for centuries. The Samaritans had built their own temple on Mount Gerizim, and used only part of the Jewish Bible. By the time of Jesus the Jews hated Samaritans and had nothing to do with them. But Jesus ministered to Samaritans, and made one of them the hero of a famous parable, the Good Samaritan (Luke 10.30-37).

Gentiles

The name Gentiles, from the Roman word for 'races', was given by Jews to all other races such as Romans and Greeks. Strict laws made sure that the people of God kept themselves pure by living apart from all non-Jews. Many Jews believed that these pagans lay outside the care of God. But prophets believed that God called his people to be 'a light to lighten the Gentiles', to make God known to them (Luke 2.25-32). Jesus ministered to Gentiles who came to him. Some Greeks and Romans admired Jewish religion, and attended services at synagogues, though they could not accept Jewish laws or become Jews. Jews had strict rules about such things as trading with Gentiles, entering a Gentile house, and eating with Gentiles. Jews in Palestine hated their Roman rulers even more because they were Gentiles and worshippers of pagan gods.

People 2

Jesus lived about 2,000 years ago. We divide history by the date of his birth. The years before it are B.C. (Before Christ). The years since his birth are A.D. (from Roman words meaning 'in the year of the Lord'). This way of dividing history was worked out in the sixth century by a monk. But he made a mistake of about five years. So Jesus was born, not exactly between 1 B.C. and 1 A.D., but five years earlier. The dates of his earthly life were from about 5 B.C. to 29 A.D.

Herod the Great

King Herod died in 4 B.C. so that he was still alive when Jesus was born. He came from the land of Edom whose people were related to Jews. But they were hated, and the Jews always regarded Herod as a foreigner. He was a clever ruler and he was made King of the Jews by the Romans. He married a Jewish princess, and rebuilt the temple at Jerusalem making it a magnificent building. But Jews still hated him. He ruled as a tyrant, and grew mad with suspicion. He had his Jewish wife and three of his sons put to death when he suspected them of plotting against him. It would be quite like him to have all baby boys at Bethlehem put to death when wise men told him that a new king had been born there (Matthew 2.1-16).

Annas and Caiaphas

The head of Jewish religion was the High Priest. He was chosen from the families of priests who controlled the temple at Jerusalem. Caiaphas was the High Priest who tried Jesus. But he first sent Jesus to Annas, his father-in-law, who was the previous High Priest and had great authority (John 18.12-14). Caiaphas was High Priest from 18 to 36 A.D., and later he tried Peter and John for preaching in the name of Jesus.

Pontius Pilate

The Roman emperor appointed a Procurator or Governor to rule over any troublesome part of his empire. Pontius Pilate was Governor of the Jews from 26 to 36 A.D. He was responsible for seeing that law and order were kept, and that Roman law was properly administered. He appointed the High Priest and controlled the Temple and its funds. He had to ratify death sentences passed by the Council of the Jews. Pilate was tactless and obstinate. He angered the Jews by such foolish acts as having Roman standards taken into the sacred Temple area: and taking money from the Temple funds for building an aqueduct to bring water from Bethlehem to Jerusalem. Only he could condemn Jesus to death and in the end he cowardly gave way to the demands of the priests for the death of Jesus, knowing him to be innocent of the charges of being a rebel (Mark 15.1-15). Pilate's blunders and obstinacy led to constant riots. He was recalled to Rome in 36 A.D. to be tried by the emperor and he died there.

Life in the time of Jesus

Herod Antipas

When Herod the Great died his kingdom was divided between his four sons. One of them named Herod Antipas ruled over Galilee where Jesus lived and taught. Herod was crafty and treacherous and superstitious. He was in Jerusalem when Pilate had to try Jesus. As soon as Pilate heard that Jesus was a Galilean he sent him to Herod to be tried by his own ruler. Herod was pleased for he had long wanted to meet Jesus. He hoped to see Jesus work wonders before him. But Jesus said nothing, and Herod had to send him back to Pilate for the case to be decided.

John the Baptist

John the Baptist was born in 7 B.C. His father was a priest, and his mother was related to Mary, the mother of Jesus. Thus John and Jesus may have been cousins. John was dedicated to God from his birth. When he grew up he knew that God had called him for a special task. He went out to live a hard and strict life in the desert. About 28 A.D. he began his ministry at a ford in the river Jordan which travellers had to cross. There he preached, calling men to repent and be baptized. He proclaimed that he was a messenger, a herald preparing the way. When his cousin Jesus came to be baptized John was humble but glad, for now his preaching would be fulfilled. Later, he openly condemned Herod for divorcing his wife and marrying his niece named Herodias. Herod, already afraid of the popular prophet, had John thrown in prison and there, to please Herodias, he had John beheaded.

Judas Iscariot

Judas Iscariot was the only one of the twelve apostles who did not come from Galilee. 'Iscariot' means 'man of Kerioth', a village in Judaea. Judas kept the money-bag for the band of disciples. His love of money may have been the reason why he betrayed Jesus to the priests for 30 pieces of silver. Some think that he had the wrong idea of the kind of Messiah that Jesus was; and that he decided to betray Jesus to force him to declare himself as the popular leader whom the Jews longed for. Whatever his reason Judas was deeply sorry for betraying Jesus, and hanged himself in his remorse (Matthew 27.3-5).

Martha and Mary

The sisters Martha and Mary lived with their brother Lazarus in the village of Bethany just outside Jerusalem. They were friends of Jesus and he stayed with them when he visited the city. It was there that Mary anointed the head of Jesus with the precious spikenard oil.

Joseph of Arimathea

Joseph of Arimathea was a disciple of Jesus, but he kept his faith secret because he was afraid of the Jewish authorities. He was a member of the Council of the Jews but, although he had not voted for the death of Jesus, fear had prevented him from speaking up for Jesus. It was only after Jesus had died on the cross that he was brave enough to show his faith. He got permission from Pilate to bury the body of Jesus in the new tomb which he had prepared for his own family.

Food

Jesus grew up in an ordinary peasant home. The family lived on home-made bread, fruits, fish, vegetables and eggs. They had milk and wine to drink.

Breakfast was a quick and simple snack, with bread, raisins, figs and olives and goat's milk to drink. Workers left home early, and often took food in their girdles to eat on the way and during the day. The second meal at midday was for rest and refreshment. The chief meal of the day was evening supper after the day's work was done. The family sat on mats or cushions round a big bowl of food which they all shared. Stew made with vegetables and sometimes meat was a favorite dish.

Rich men followed the Greek and Roman custom of reclining on couches for meals (Luke 7.36-8). They leaned on the left arm and ate food with the right hand. But all Jews kept the food laws of their people, for they were part of the sacred laws in their Bible. They were strict rules of hygiene for choosing, preparing and cooking food, and they were part of Jewish religion. Still today Jewish food must be 'kosher' or 'proper', prepared properly according to the sacred food laws.

Bread

Bread was the most important part of every meal. In the Hebrew language of the Jews 'to eat bread' meant 'to have a meal'. Only rich men could afford bread made with wheat. Peasants had barley-bread. The housewife had to bake bread each day, for bread quickly turns mouldy in a hot land. Grinding the grain between the two mill-stones was hard work, best done by two women together (Luke 17.35). Few could afford corn already ground by mules or oxen working a grinding-machine.

After grinding the meal was mixed with salt and water to make dough. This would be cooked to make unleavened bread. To make the dough rise women used fermented dough left from the last baking – but only a little of this leaven was needed (Luke 13.20-1).

The small round loaves could be baked simply on an earthenware plate heated by a fire underneath. A proper oven was made of clay, shaped like a bell, with the fire at the bottom. The flat cakes of dough were placed on top, or stuck to the inside when the fire was removed.

The little loaves were broken with the fingers, not cut with a knife (Mark 14.22). Food was picked out of the common dish with fingers. A piece of bread was used like a spoon to sop up the rich gravy from the bowl (John 13.26).

146

Life in the time of Jesus

Drinks

In a hot land like Israel it is a matter of life and death to have enough to drink. Rains came twice a year, but there were few reservoirs to store water. The rains came in violent storms in a few days. But the torrents rushed away leaving dried-up riverbeds. The only sure water was from wells and springs and streams.

Most families owned one of the common goats. It gave them milk to drink and cheese made from it. Most had a sheep too, kept for its milk and wool. Milk did not stay fresh for long in the heat. But people were used to thicker sour milk and found it better than fresh milk for quenching thirst.

Some drinks were made from fruits, and a beer was made from barley. But wine was the most popular drink of all. Vines grew easily in the land of Jesus. They trailed over the ground, held up by props, or through fruit trees. Every vineyard had a watch-tower for a man to guard the growing vines from thieves and jackals and little foxes. When grape-harvest was near whole families camped in the vineyards, ready to cut the bunches with small pruning-hooks. Then donkeys laden with full baskets carried the grapes to the winepress.

Some grapes were eaten fresh, some put aside for drying into raisins, and some boiled to make grape-honey – for sugar was unknown. The rest went into the wine-press, a pit dug in the earth or cut out of the soft limestone rock. All joined in trampling the grapes with bare feet, singing as they worked. The juice ran into a deeper trough and was left until stalks and skins sank to the bottom. Then the wine was drawn off and stored in new winejars or wineskins and sealed (Mark 2.22). Water was added to the red wine to make the popular drink that was regarded as a gift from God.

Olives

Old gnarled olive-trees were very common. They grew to a good height in dry, stony soil and lived to a great age. Olive-harvest in October ended the year on the land. Fruits for eating were picked while the olives were still green, and they were preserved in salt water. The rest were beaten from the trees with long rods, when fully ripe, and gathered in baskets for the oil-press.

Some olives were not pressed but only bruised, and left for the oil to drip from them. This was the best oil, used as holy oil for worship and for anointing the sick (Mark 6.13). Most were pressed in an oil-press, made from a beam wedged in the rock and weighted with stones. As the fruit was pressed the oil dripped into basins and was later stored in clay jars.

Olive oil had many uses. It was used for cooking, for making light in clay oil-lamps, for making perfumes and ointments and medicines. A single olive tree gave enough oil to last a family for the whole year. Some farmers kept many olive trees. A hill outside Jerusalem was called Mount of Olives from its olive-orchard. Jesus went there with his disciples and into a garden called Gethsemane or Oil Press, for the olives were pressed there (Mark 14.26-32).

Other Fruits

Fig trees were as common as vines and olive trees. A fig tree lived to a great age and gave three crops each year. The bursting buds of the common fig tree were the first sign of summer. The thick leaves gave fine shade for rest from the sun (John 1.48).

Dates were popular. They were eaten fresh, and also used to make cakes with a sweet taste. Date trees grew in well-watered places like Jericho, called City of Palm Trees. Men had to climb up their tall trunks to gather the golden-brown clusters of dates. Palm leaves were used in religious festivals and processions (John 12.12-13).

Pomegranates grew freely near Cana, a town in Galilee that Jesus knew (John 2.1-2). The round rose-red fruits with their many seeds gave a bitter red juice used for drinks and for medicines. Walkers, like Jesus and his disciples, would find them refreshing on a hot day.

fig   *pomegranate*   *dates*

Salt

The Jews were fond of seasoning their food with herbs and spices. They used mustard, mint, coriander, saffron, cummin, and rue to give flavor to food. They used walnuts, almonds and pistachio nuts too. Only wealthy men could afford pepper or cinnamon imported from distant lands. Peasant people were fond of garlic, onions and shallots. Wealthy people flavored their wines as well as food.

But everyone, rich or poor, needed salt. No one could live without it. We understand now why the body needs salt, especially in hot lands where it is lost through perspiring.

Salt is also precious for preserving foods, especially in hot lands where it quickly goes bad. Salt came from the Dead Sea, also called the Salt Sea. Salt was dug from the cliffs around it, or collected in large pans simply by letting water from the Dead Sea evaporate. Jews needed salt to season their vegetables, and to preserve foods such as fish and vegetables and olives.

Meat and Poultry

The sacred food laws permitted eating meat only from 'clean' animals: those which had divided hooves and chew the cud, such as sheep, goats, oxen. Unclean or forbidden animals are those which do not have cloven hooves, do not walk on their hooves, do not chew the cud, such as camels, pigs, dogs, cats. Both meat and milk from unclean animals were forbidden. Greeks and Romans were fond of pigs' meat, and used pigs for sacrifices to their Gods. Jews would have nothing to do with pigs or their meat. To be a swineherd was a terrible disgrace as well as breaking the sacred law (Luke 15.13-16).

Peasant people could not often afford meat. The lamb at Passover, roasted on a spit over an open fire, was very special. Most peasant meat came from the young of goats which were common and cheap. Only for a special time, like a wedding or birthday or feast, was a sheep killed for meat. Its broad tail was a rare delicacy, as well as providing lots of fat to be put away for winter.

'Clean' birds which could be eaten were hens, geese, partridge, quail and pigeons. The food laws forbade the meat of birds of prey.

Life in the time of Jesus

Fish

Fish was a vital food, especially for peasants who could not afford much meat. Fishing was a big industry around the Sea of Galilee, with its many fishing towns and villages. The most common fish from its warm waters were carp, perch, bream and the little 'St Peter's fish'. For these were 'clean' fish, with scales and fins. Forbidden fish were eels, shellfish, and every kind of creeping creature, such as crabs, lobsters, snails and oysters. Much of the catch from the Sea of Galilee was quickly salted and sent to towns such as Jerusalem, which had a fish-market and a Fish-Gate into the city. Salted fish from Galilee was exported to Rome, and even to faraway Spain. Four of the fishermen were called by Jesus to be 'fishers of men' (Mark 2.16-20).

Vegetables

Vegetables were an important part of the diet of Jews in the time of Jesus. The most common were beans, lentils, peas, lettuce, cucumber, squash, onions and garlic. From them was made the rich stew that was the favorite dish of a family when they gathered for supper.

149

Children

The Jews loved children. It was almost a disgrace not to marry, and it was even worse to be married and to have no children. The birth of a child was celebrated with ancient customs and with great joy, especially if the first baby was a boy. On the eighth day a Jewish baby boy was circumcised. This was a small operation on his penis and was the mark of a Jew. It was the outward sign of being one of the people of God. The baby boy was given his name at this ceremony too.

Boys and girls began their education at home, learning the ways and beliefs of their people from their mothers and fathers. Many everyday events had a religious meaning. Special days were observed at home – the Sabbath day each week, and the feast days and fast days during the year. Children learned about God and his laws from their parents. They learned some psalms and prayers and texts by heart. Each child had a special text which contained the letters of his or her own name.

Schools

In the time of Jesus the Jews had compulsory education, just as we do today. But only boys went to school, while girls were taught by their mothers at home. Boys began school at 6 years of age and finished when they became 12 years of age. Their 'text books' were the sacred writings of their Bible. They were written in Hebrew, the language of Jews. But the people spoke a language called Aramaic. So boys had to learn the Hebrew alphabet and to practice its letters before they could read and write in Hebrew.

Big towns had proper schoolrooms, but most schools were held at the local synagogue. The boys met there in the courtyard. They sat in a circle round their teacher and practiced their letters in the sand. Then they could begin to read and to study the sacred books.

Sometimes a Scribe, an expert in the holy writings, visited the school. He would question the older boys, and discuss with them the meaning of the sacred books.

But school did not go on all day. Boys had to learn a trade so as to be able to earn their living when they grew up. Most boys learned the craft or trade of their own fathers. So a boy would be busy each day working alongside his father, learning his trade or craft.

While the boys were at school their sisters learned by helping their mothers at home.

Life in the time of Jesus

Toys

Jewish children had toys like those children have today. But there was one difference. The sacred law of Moses forbade making any 'graven images'. So the dolls given to girls had no faces on them. Some of them were simply rag dolls. But others, made of terra cotta, had arms and legs with joints so that they could be worked with strings like our puppets. Girls had model furniture just as girls do today in their dolls' houses. There was plenty of clay to shape animals and make model farms.

Whipping tops were common and so were dice, knuckle-bones, and a game like our draughts. Some children were lucky enough to have wooden horses and swings.

Games

Children who were not lucky enough to have many toys of their own could always make up games. They often played ball games, though they did not have bats. They hit the ball with their hands, as we do in the game of fives. Younger children played hide-and-seek, hop-scotch, and chasing games. Older children played guessing games and charades. Boys enjoyed making pipes out of reeds.

Jewish boys and girls, like all children, imitated grown-ups in their play. Best of all was playing at weddings and funerals, acting out what they had seen happen at these ceremonies. All the boys and girls could join in, and there was plenty of room in the market-place of the town. There was dressing up, and making music with pipes and drums, rattles and clappers. There was dancing and singing, stamping and clapping, laughing and wailing.

Family Life

Jewish religion came into every part of daily life in Palestine. There were special laws about food, about meals, and even about the correct way to entertain visitors. There were many festivals during the year, as well as the weekly sabbath. Besides religious festivals there were special celebrations after each crop had been harvested. Happiest of all were marriage festivities, lasting several days, to which everyone was invited.

Family Life

The father was head of the family and he had complete authority. On his death the eldest son received the largest share of the property and took over as head of the family. This was the birth right. Younger sons had to make their own way in life.

Women were responsible for running the home, cooking, spinning and weaving to make clothes, and fetching water and wood. Water was scarce for there were few reservoirs. In the big towns water-sellers went round the streets.

Eating

Before eating their main meal the family gathered in a circle, sitting on mats. First came the ritual washing of hands and a short grace. Then the meal began.

There were no plates or knives or forks. The food was served in a big bowl, placed in the center, and everyone helped himself using his right hand only (Mark 14.20). Bread was eaten with the meal, and it was broken up into small pieces. They could be used as spoons to dip into the bowl.

Birth

Children were very important in Jewish religion. They were 'gifts from God'; and to be childless was a disgrace – it might even be thought a punishment for sin. The law allowed divorce for a man, and it was easy to obtain. But divorce was not allowed to a woman. A childless wife might easily be divorced by her husband. Then she was destitute and her life was as sad as that of widows.

Children were greatly loved and well cared for; and male children were eagerly awaited as heirs. The first-born son was heir, so if twins were born the doctor decided which came first. If a husband died with no heirs it was an old custom for his brother to marry the widow to provide an heir for his estate and to preserve his name.

The rules of the sabbath could be overlooked by the doctor and midwife at a birth. The newborn baby was washed, and rubbed with salt which was believed to toughen the skin. Then it was tightly wrapped in swaddling clothes for the first few days, wound round it like bandages (Luke 2.7). That would make the limbs grow straight, people believed. The manger in the house, used by the animals at night, made a fine cradle for the baby during the day.

152

Life in the time of Jesus

Marriage

Weddings were very happy times, with the celebrations lasting for a week. They usually came when harvest was gathered in, and everyone was free from work. Marriages were arranged by parents, and their children were married at a very young age.

First the bridegroom's parents chose the bride, and then made a dowry, a gift of money, to her parents.

Then came the betrothal ceremony, when the young couple made their solemn promises to each other before their parents and two witnesses. For being betrothed was as binding as being married. Rings were exchanged and the engaged couple then received the blessing of their parents.

After a year of betrothal came the wedding celebrations. A procession of the bridegroom's friends, lit by the lamps of the bridesmaids, escorted the bride from her parents' home to the house of her husband. The bride brought her belongings with her, her clothes and what jewellery she had. If her family were well-to-do she might bring a gift of land as well. There was much singing and dancing in the procession, with all the villagers following on and joining in. Flowers and nuts were thrown over the couple. They sat together under a canopy at the feast and shared their meal; for sharing food always bound people together. The festivities, held at the house of the bridegroom's parents, went on throughout the week. Then the young couple set up home together.

Death

Burial took place within 24 hours of death. This was wise in a hot country like Palestine, and it is another example of the sound reasoning behind so many Jewish laws. The body was washed, anointed with oils and spices, and bound with burial cloths. Tombs were usually caves cut into the soft limestone rocks, with a big boulder to cover the entrance.

Music

Music played a large part in all ceremonies – especially in weddings, funerals, and all the religious and agricultural festivals. It was accompanied by singing and dancing, clapping hands and stamping feet. The instruments used were simple. There were many forms of stringed instruments, especially the harp and lute and lyre.

The main wind instruments were trumpets, and simple flutes and pipes. The rhythm was made with drums, tambourines, and small cup-shaped finger cymbals. Small orchestras were formed for combining these sounds with choirs.

Jews and Gentiles

All people who did not share the religion of Jews were called Gentiles. Many laws were concerned with how Jews should behave towards them. Because Gentiles worshipped pagan gods the Jews believed that they would be tainted by contact with them. It would make them spiritually impure.

If a Jew entered the house of a Gentile, even to offer help in an emergency, he was unclean until the evening. If a Gentile entered a Jewish house he must not be left alone in the room.

It was against the laws to let or sell houses or land to Gentiles, for they might be used for heathen worship, or the land made the site for a heathen temple. Jews had to suspend all forms of trading with Gentiles when one of their heathen festivals was near. For they might indirectly be aiding or financing the festival by their trading.

153

Animals

Palestine was much more fertile in Bible times than it is now, with many animals roaming wild. Around the River Jordan there were thick forests where lived jungle animals like lions, leopards and jungle-cats. They were fewer by the time of Jesus. Many trees had been cut down, and many wild animals had been captured to fight with the gladiators in Roman arenas. Jews kept many domestic animals – for work, for food and drink, and for skins. Their food laws made them shun 'unclean' animals.

Birds

There were about 300 different kinds of birds in Palestine. Among the most common were turtle-doves, partridge, hawks and owls. Eagles and vultures were well known too. Migrating birds included swallows, herons, storks, cranes, and the quails which were popular for their rich meat.

Domestic Animals

Oxen, asses and donkeys were kept as working animals. Oxen were very strong but costly. A poor farmer with only one ox would yoke it with an ass to pull his plough. Donkeys were used to turn wheels, and to carry big loads. People rode on donkeys and even a poor family had one. Horses were costly and rare. Roman officers rode on horses, and they were animals of war. Merchants used one-humped camels in trains for crossing the desert. With water and food stored in their bodies, and carrying heavy loads, they could travel 30 miles in a day. Goats were as common as sheep and they mixed together in the herds. Even a poor family had a goat for milk, butter and cheese. Goat hair was woven to make clothes and tent-cloth. Goat skins made bottles, sandals, slings and rough garments. Goat horns were used for carrying oil. Sheep were kept for their fine wool and their milk.

Other Animals

The wild goats with long horns, called ibex, were common. There was the dangerous wild boar and wild ox too. Other large animals were antelope and gazelles. Smaller animals included mice, hares, hedgehogs and porcupines. Out in the hot dry wilderness were snakes and scorpions and lizards. Among common insects were butterflies, grasshoppers, and the locusts whose swarms were dreaded by farmers.

Predators

Shepherds had to be on constant watch for animals like jackals, wolves, Syrian bears, even lions and leopards, which came after their sheep. Watchmen had to guard the ripening grapes in vineyards, and chickens on the farms, from foxes and jackals (Luke 9.58). Jews did not keep dogs as pets. Hyenas and wild dogs were 'unclean' and they ran wild, scavenging for food.

Medicine

In ancient times men did not have our modern knowledge of medicine. But peoples like the Babylonians, Egyptians, Greeks and Romans knew a great deal about the art of healing. They had surgeons, doctors, dentists, hospitals and medicines.
People everywhere believed that healing came from their gods. Priests were doctors, and their temples were hospitals. Sickness and disease came from the powers of evil, from devils. They could also be sent by the gods as a punishment for wrong-doing.

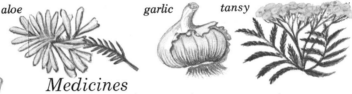

aloe garlic tansy

Health Laws

The health laws of the Jews are included in their Bible as part of their religion. There are strict laws for choosing and preparing and cooking food; for personal hygiene, keeping the body clean; for men and for women; and for disease spreading among the people.

A man with a contagious disease like leprosy could be sent into quarantine by the priest. This was not the sickness we call leprosy but a skin disease that could clear up. If the man thought that it had healed he had to show himself to the priest who would decide whether he could go back home (Matthew 8.2-4).

The law against touching a dead body was like that too, for the body might carry disease. In the parable of the Good Samaritan, told by Jesus, a Priest and a Levite took one look at the wounded man lying in the road and hurried past. They were keeping the sacred law, for the man might be dead (Luke 10.30-32). Besides, God might be punishing him for his sins.

Medicines

In that parable of Jesus it was the Good Samaritan who helped the wounded man, first bathing his wounds with wine and oil (Luke 10.33-34). The wine would act as an antiseptic cleaning his wounds. The oil would soothe the wounds and help them to heal.

Jews had many medicines and a special prescription for each kind of ailment. Their medicines came from herbs and spices, from fruits and leaves, from minerals and wines. Many of these 'folk medicines' were similar to drugs used today. A famous balm, from the gum of a certain bush, was prized everywhere for its healing powers. Poultices for boils were made from figs. Mineral springs and rivers were known for their healing properties.

Mind and Body

In ancient times men realised that illness often came from the mind. So the way to cure the body was first to heal the mind.

There were many wonder-workers claiming to perform miracles of healing with their magic potions and spells and charms. Many sick people were brought to Jesus. He healed their minds and bodies out of compassion for them, bidding them not to broadcast what had happened. For his healings were not wonders to make people marvel. They were signs of God's loving power. His kingdom had come in Jesus and those who saw these signs should seek to enter God's kingdom.

Index

Emmaus 124
Galilee 8, 25, 93
Gethsemane 114
Jericho 16, 75
Jerusalem 9, 14, 75, 102
Mount Carmel 13
Mount Hermon 13, 99, 101
Mount of Olives 114, 147
Nazareth 8, 13, 24
Phoenicia 99, 108
Sea of Galilee 93
Tiberias 58
Tyre 108

Religious Customs

Abba 17
alms-giving 89
baptizing 19
burying 123
Council of the Jews 122
Covenant (or Testament) 114
dedicating a baby 12

fasting 90
Feast of Lights 102, 137
Feast of Passover 14, 104, 113, 137
Feast of Pentecost 127, 137
Feast of Tabernacles 101, 137
hallelujahs 16
mourning 58
praying 54
signs of sorrow for sin 90
synagogue 14, 24, 52, 138
Temple of Jerusalem 14, 16, 22, 54, 75, 107, 136
tithing 54
washing 88

Romans

Roman census 9, 134
Roman emperor 134
Roman roads 13, 134
Roman rule 8, 134
Roman soldiers 141, 134
Roman taxes 9, 21, 27, 110, 134

Spices and Scents

aloes 123
frankincense 12
myrrh 12, 123
oil for anointing head 104
spikenard 105

Water

aqueduct 86
bottles 38
rains 51, 147
skins 48

Work

carpentry 91
farming 25
fishing 132
shepherding 37, 131
stewards 80
swineherd 32
unemployment 49, 133
vine-growing 131

STORIES JESUS TOLD
Stories called Parables

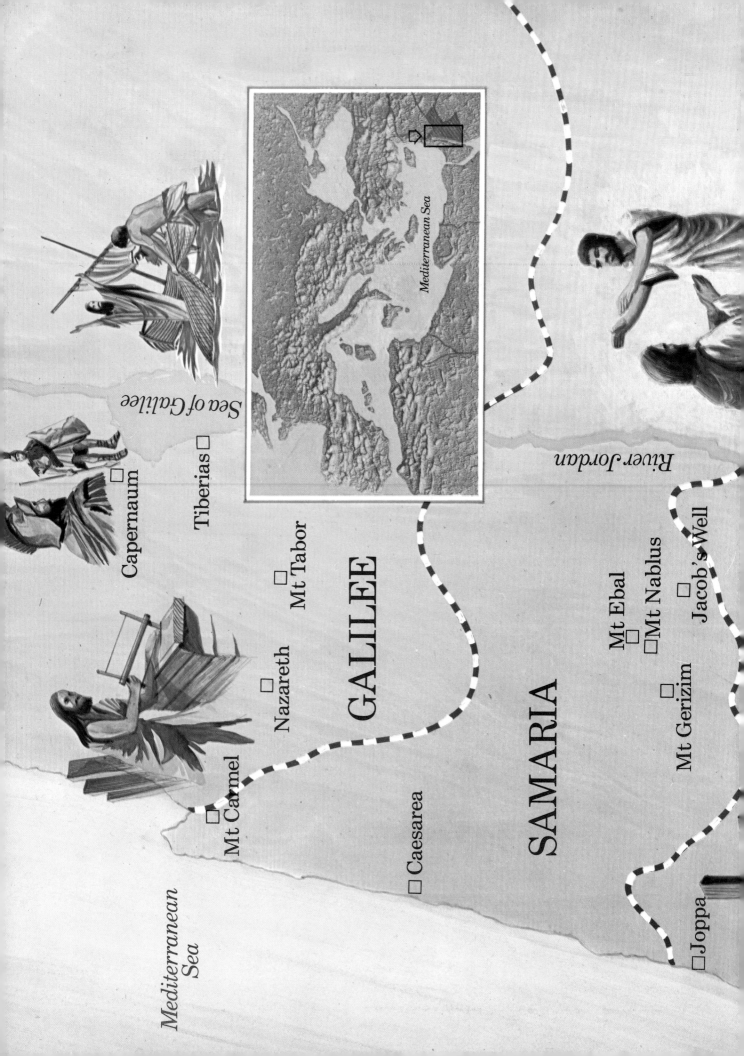

Mediterranean Sea

Sea of Galilee

Capernaum

Tiberias

Mt Tabor

Nazareth

GALILEE

Mt Carmel

Caesarea

SAMARIA

Mt Ebal

Mt Nablus

Jacob's Well

Mt Gerizim

River Jordan

Joppa

Mediterranean Sea